A Short Course in Teaching Reading Skills

Beatrice S. Mikulecky

Addison-Wesley Publishing Company

Reading, Massachusetts • Menlo Park, California • New York
Don Mills, Ontario • Wokingham, England • Amsterdam • Bonn
Sydney • Singapore • Tokyo • Madrid • San Juan

A Publication of the World Language Division
Editorial: Kathleen Sands-Boehmer and Karen Doyle
Manufacturing/Production: James W. Gibbons
Interior Design: Herb Caswell
Cover Design: Prentice Crosier

Pages 50–51 reprinted courtesy of *The Boston Globe*; pp. 142–143 from *Developing Reading Skills* by Francoise Grellet, © 1981, Cambridge University Press. Reprinted with permission; p. 46 from *Impact! Student Book 1*, p. from *Impact! Teacher's Guide 1*, pp. 46–47 from *Impact! Student Book 2* all by Janice Motta and Kathryn Riley, © 1982 by Addison-Wesley Publishing Company, Reading MA; p. 1 from *The Journal of Verbal Learning and Verbal Behavior Volume 11* by John D. Bransford and Maria K. Johnson, © 1972; p. 137 reprinted by permission of Beatrice Mikulecky; pp. 78, 133 reprinted by permission of Elizabeth Mikulecky; p. 39 from *Nisa: The Life and Words of a !Kung Woman* by Marjorie Shostak © 1983 Random House/Vintage Books; p. 53 reprinted by permission from *Reading Laboratory Kit 3A* by Don H. Parker. © 1973 by Science Research Associates, Inc.; pp. 40, 47, 48, 52, 55, 70, 74, 83, 90, 92, 97, 105, 108–109, 116–117, 119–120, 124, 132, 141–142, 144 from *Reading Power* by Beatrice Mikulecky and Linda Jeffries © 1986 Addison-Wesley Publishing Company, Reading, MA; pp. 125–126, 130–131 reprinted from *Reading and Thinking in English: Exploring Functions* by John Moore et al, © 1979 Oxford University Press; p. 75 from *Skillful Reading: A Text and Workbook for Students of English as a Second Language* by Amy L. Sonka, © 1981. Reprinted by permission of Prentice-Hall, Inc., Englewood Cliffs, N.J.; p. 140 from *Skimming and Scanning* by Edward Fry, © 1978 Jamestown Publishers, Providence, Rhode Island. Reprinted by permission; pp. 102–103, 106–108 from *Tactics in Reading I* by O. Niles, D. Bracken, M. Dougherty, and R. Kinder. © 1965 by Scott, Foresman and Co. Reprinted by permission; pp. 94–96, 129–130 from *Tactics in Reading II* by O. Niles, D. Bracken, M. Dougherty, and R. Kinder. © 1965 by Scott, Foresman and Co. Reprinted by permission; pp. 134–135 from *Tactics in Reading III* by O. Niles. © 1967 by Scott, Foresman and Co. Reprinted by permission; p. 87 from *Thirty Lessons in Outlining* by E. Ross and T. Culliton. © 1971 Curriculum Associates, Inc. Reproduced by permission of the publisher; p. 74 from *The Theater Arts and the Teaching of Second Language* by Stephen Smith. © 1984 Addison-Wesley Publishing Co., Reading, MA; pp. 56–57 from *Timed Readings* by E. Spargo and G. Williston. © 1980 Jamestown Publishers, Providence, Rhode Island. Reprinted by permission.

ISBN 0-201-50079-5

14 15 16 17 18 19 – CRS – 070605040302

Mikulecky, Beatrice S.
  A short course in teaching reading skills/Beatrice S. Mikulecky.
      p.   cm.
  Bibliography: p.
  Includes index.
  ISBN 0-201-50079-5
  1. English language — Study and teaching — Foreign speakers.
2. Reading comprehension. 3. Books and reading. I. Title.
PE1128.A2M55   1989
428.4'07 — dc20   89-32002
                                                                  CIP

Contents

PART III

Contents

Introduction

WHO IS THIS BOOK FOR?

This book is intended for classroom teachers who have always wished that they could do more for their students in the way of reading comprehension instruction. It presents a brief overview of the theory and practice of teaching reading, with special emphasis on meeting the needs of students of English as a second or foreign language and other limited English proficient students. The principles outlined apply to students of any age and language proficiency level who already have basic decoding abilities.

You will find that the approach and methods of teaching reading described and explained in this book can benefit several different kinds of students:

- ESL (English as a Second Language) students can learn to read and think in English as they are expected to in schools in English-speaking countries.

- EFL (English as a Foreign Language) students living in non-English speaking countries usually rely on written texts for "immersion" in English. They can learn to read with the thinking skills needed to read widely and deeply in English.

- LEP (Limited English Proficient) students may speak English fluently, but their home language is not mainstream, standard English. Through the approach detailed in this book, they can master mainstream literacy skills.

- Students who possess language processing disabilities (such as dyslexia) often benefit from the structured, developmental approach found here.

- Non-"mainstream" students in junior or community colleges often need to develop the reading skills discussed in this book in order to succeed in their college courses.

- Adult native speakers of English who are attending literacy centers and other adult basic education (ABE) programs can acquire advanced reading and thinking skills which are required for further job training programs and diploma examinations through the approach and methods this book outlines.

BACKGROUND

In the last ten years or so, the teaching of reading has emerged as an important component of language instruction, especially in the United States and England, judging from the many books and articles which have been published on the subject. Besides numerous articles in journals, excellent books have been published which focus on the principles and techniques of teaching reading in a second language (Cates and Swaffar, 1979; Dubin, Eskey and Grabe, 1986; Grellet, 1981; Hudelson, 1981; Mackay, Barkman and Jordan, 1979; Nuttall, 1982). In addition, a new journal, *Reading in a Foreign Language* has been published in England since 1983.

The renewed interest in the teaching of reading in ESL/EFL can be traced to several sources. First, research in psycholinguistics and cognitive psychology has resulted in great advances in understanding the reading process. Such research was carried out by, to name a few, Anderson, Brown, Goodman, Kintsch, Meyer, Rumelhart, and Smith. Although first language reading and related research was more or less ignored by second language professionals for many years, a few second language researchers have recently been studying its applicability to second language reading processes, including Alderson, Carrell, Clarke, Connor, Eskey, Grabe, Stoller, and others. They have found that second language professionals can learn a lot from first language reading research. Increased contact with researchers and teachers from non-English-speaking countries, where reading is stressed in the foreign language classroom (for example at TESOL Conventions), has strengthened this point of view.

Another reason for a greater interest in teaching reading is that literacy in both first and second languages has become a burning issue in many parts of the world. One important factor is the immigration of large numbers of refugees from third world countries into highly industrialized nations and the resettlement of cultural groups in several parts of the world, which have high-lighted a problem faced by language teachers everywhere. In the United States, many school districts have established classes for students labeled "limited English proficient." These students may have been born in the United States, but at home, the family language is not standard English. Indeed, LEP students are learning standard English as a "second" language.

In some countries where English is taught as a foreign language (such as Israel, Finland, and Sweden), reading has traditionally been an integral part of the language course. And as English has developed into a world language, students, researchers, business people, and many others have had to learn to read well in English in order to have access to materials available only in English.

However, many teacher training programs in the United States have not included courses in the theories and methods of reading instruction. In fact, the teaching of reading in ESL/EFL has often been downplayed. One can only speculate about the reasons for the lack of "status" of reading as a separate component of second language instruction. Perhaps many teachers, unschooled in contemporary reading theory, were trying to get away from what they regarded as translation approaches to acquiring English. And some conscientious teachers may have assumed that reading skills all transfer auto-matically from the first language. (This may or may not be the case. . . .see Alderson, 1984; Coady, 1977). Moreover, many otherwise excellent books and articles about theories of the reading process often do not make a clear connection between theory and classroom practice.

Therefore, a paradoxical situation exists in language classrooms in the United States and in many other countries. Although most instructional materials require reading, there is very little systematic instruction in how to comprehend texts.

An emphasis on reading instruction can enhance the acquisition of stan-dard English in many ways, including:

- an increased awareness of the language (metalinguistic awareness);
- immersion in the second language, resulting in increased acquisition;
- models for improving writing in English;
- success in academic studies;
- improved vocabulary;
- increased cultural background knowledge;
- the transfer of some first language reading skills;
- improvement of first language reading abilities.

Today, as many English teachers recognize the importance of reading instruction, they are looking for new, effective ways to teach reading. But simple "recipes" are not enough. When their teaching is based on an understanding of underlying theories of reading and literacy development, teachers can be more confident and can plan more coherent lessons. Therefore, some connections need to be made between theory and classroom practice.

CONTENTS OF THIS BOOK

The book is divided into three parts. Part I contains a definition and a model of the reading comprehension process; a brief summary of recent advances in understanding the concept of literacy; a discussion of the connections between literacy and reading comprehension; a look at the cultural aspects of reading comprehension; an overview of the components of an effective reading course; and an explanation of a general teaching methodology which is based on recent educational research.

Part II presents a method for individualizing student pleasure reading. It also details ideas for promoting the ways of thinking and speaking which are necessary for developing literate skills in English.

Part III contains descriptions of some key reading skills, their relationships to the theory presented in Part I, and a methodology and rationale for teaching them. This part consists primarily of sample skills lessons.

An Appendix and a comprehensive Bibliography appear at the end of the book.

Acknowledgements

Talking about what you are writing is essential. I had the good fortune of having conversations with many thoughtful, stimulating people while writing this book, including Paul Abraham, Nancy Carroll, Jim Gee, Daniel Giese, Ann Hilferty, Steve Molinsky, Tom Rowe, Ann Marie Speicher, Fredericka Stoller, Margot Valdivia, and Janette-Yael Zupnik. I would like to thank the following reviewers for their comments on the manuscript: Sheila Fischer, Alemany Community College; M. Eileen Hansen, Middlesex County College; Maryann O'Brien, University of Houston, Fredricka Stoller, Northern Arizona University and Janette-Yael Zupnik, Boston University. I also wish to express my appreciation to Kathy Sands-Boehmer at Addison-Wesley. And for their continued caring and encouragement, special thanks go to Liz Mikulecky and Jim Mackay.

PART I | Reading and Literacy: Some Connections

It seems logical that a book on teaching reading should begin with a section which includes a discussion of literacy, since recent research has shown that the social contexts of literacy are the basis of the acquisition of reading and writing. Social contexts include the student's cultural background, prior knowledge, and language style, as well as the settings in which reading and writing are used and taught. In this section, we will connect these ideas to the teaching of reading. We will define reading and literacy, examine the relationships between the two concepts, and outline some implications for teaching reading to ESL, EFL, and other LEP students.

WHAT IS READING?

At the outset, let us agree on what we mean by reading. In order to do so, please read the passage which follows. What is it about and how do you know?

> A newspaper is better than a magazine. A seashore is a better place than the street. At first it is better to run than to walk. You may have to try several times. It takes some skill, but it's easy to learn. Even young children can enjoy it. Once successful, complications are minimal. Birds seldom get too close. Rain, however, soaks in very fast. Too many people doing the same thing can also cause problems. One needs lots of room. If there are no complications, it can be very peaceful. A rock will serve as an anchor. If things break loose, however, you will not get a second chance.
>
> (Bransford and Johnson, 1972)

What is the passage about?
(The answer is on the bottom of the next page.)

As a fluent reader of English, you probably engaged in the following activities while you were reading:

Sampling the text for clues to meaning.

Predicting, on the basis of the relationship between those clues and what you already know, what the meaning of the text might be and what will come next.

Testing this guess by further sampling of the text.

Confirming your guess, or rejecting it and seeking another hypothesis about what the text means.

Goodman (1970) has called this a psycholinguistic guessing game.

More specifically, you were consciously and unconsciously thinking in the ways which are described below:

Strategies of Fluent Readers

1. You noticed the distinctive features in letters, words, and meanings.

2. You guessed and took risks to predict meaning.

3. You read to identify meaning rather than to identify individual letters or words.

4. You took an active role and applied your knowledge of the world and of the topic in attempting to understand.

5. You read as though you expected the text to make sense.

6. You made use of redundancies — orthographic, syntactic, and semantic — to reduce uncertainty about meaning.

7. You maintained enough speed to overcome the limitations of visual processing and memory systems.

8. You constantly switched back and forth between the text and what you already know in an effort to understand.

(Adapted from Cooper and Petrosky, 1976)

In figuring out what the passage was about, you had to guess, because the topic was not stated. You probably had no difficulty with the vocabulary or the sentence structure. You probably made several unsuccessful guesses before you finally came up with a topic which did not seem to be contradicted by anything you could find in the text. Where *did* you finally locate the topic? It was in your own mind, of course!

The Reading Process

Let us define reading here as more than an interaction between a reader and a text (Johnston 1983:1). In most cases, especially in academic settings, a reader expects a text to make sense, hence, for the purposes of this book, which is intended for **teachers**, we are not interested in non-meaningful reading. Reading, for us, will be defined as practically synonymous with reading comprehension. Johnston (1983:17) defines this as "a complex behavior which involves conscious and unconscious use of various strategies, including problem-solving strategies, to build a model of the meaning which the writer is assumed to have intended."

It is important to reiterate the fact that until recently, much research in first language reading has been ignored by second language professionals. Yet much of that L1 research has recently been shown to be useful in understanding L2 reading and how to teach it. (i.e. Carrell 1984, 1985, 1987).

Some researchers (i.e. Kintsch and van Dijk, 1978; Rumelhart and Ortony, 1977; Winograd, 1977) have applied an information processing analogy to try to understand how people think, learn, and remember. Since reading and thinking are so thoroughly intertwir.d, this metaphor is helpful in trying to understand the reading process.

When a person reads, two aspects of the "human information processing system" continuously interact. When the reader focuses primarily on what is already known in trying to comprehend a text, this strategy is called a concept-driven or "top-down" mode. On the other hand, when the reader relies primarily on textual information to comprehend, this strategy is called a data-driven or "bottom-up" mode (Rumelhart, 1980).

In practice, these two processing strategies are employed interactively and simultaneously as the reader tries to relate the new information in the text to what is already known. But the two modes are not used equally. According to Stanovich's interactive compensatory model of reading, "a deficit in any

Answer: Making and flying a kite.

knowledge source results in a heavier reliance on other knowledge sources, regardless of the level in the processing hierarchy" (1980:63). In other words, a reader will rely on knowledge about a known topic to sort out word meaning; conversely, a reader who has a mastery of the text's vocabulary but is unfamiliar with the topic will rely on word knowledge in order to comprehend a text.

Diagram I

Model of the Reading Comprehension Process

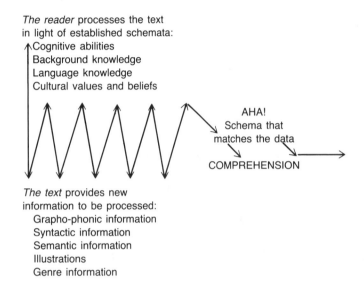

The reader constructs the meaning of the text by interpreting textual information in the light of prior knowledge and experience.

The reader is represented at the top of the diagram. When reading the text (shown at the bottom of the diagram), the reader samples the printed material (arrow pointing down) and instantaneously compares the data with what is already known (arrow pointing up), trying to find a match. The textual information activates prior knowledge, and the prior knowledge, in turn, activates expectations about what is in the text. This primarily unconscious, interactive process continues until the reader is satisfied with the match between text and prior knowledge, and comprehension has occurred (AHA!).

Diagram I summarizes an understanding of the reading process which is the result of research in psycholinguistics and cognitive science. Based on contributions from Goodman (1977), Rumelhart (1980), Smith (1973) and others, the diagram shows the following:

A. *The text.* The text (bottom portion of the figure) can be seen as a set of graphic clues to the author's intended meaning. The reader obtains samples of the text at many levels of language simultaneously. The reader notices letters, words, associated meanings, sentence structure, typographical differences, discourse structure, genre, context, and more. The reader continues to sample the text and seek mental representations (schemata) which relate to the data until a tentative match is found between the textual data and what is known.

Second language readers, especially beginners, often rely heavily on the text, especially on one level of language: words (Coady 1979). Reading and translating, word-by-word, they try to put the words together to make sense of the text. This is natural (Stanovich 1980). Until readers have acquired what Grabe terms a "critical mass" of language knowledge (1986), they will read by focusing on words.

But relying primarily on the text (bottom-up processing) will not always result in a successful interpretation of the author's intended meaning, because the author has made assumptions about the background knowledge that a reader will bring to the text. For example, when you read the "opaque" passage at the beginning of this section, you supplied the topic from your own background knowledge. There was no way that you could make sense of the passage on the word or sentence level.

B. *The Reader.* The reader, represented at the top of Diagram I, possesess the cognitive and perceptual skills needed to reason and form conceptual structures. In addition, the reader brings to the text all kinds of knowledge about the world. But the reader's mind should not be imagined as a storehouse of bits of randomly-stored information. According to cognitive theory, the mind contains whole systems of interrelated mental structures often referred to as *schemata* (Rumelhart 1977).

A schema is a general idea about a set of similar or related concepts. For example, the schema you have for school consists of all the experiences you have ever had or learned about connected with school. When you are confronted with a situation which you identify as a school (or school-like), the connections in your school schema apply, and you know what to expect and how to behave. (See Winograd 1977. Additional examples of schemata and a more detailed explanation may be found in the Appendix.)

All readers have built up conceptual frameworks (schemata) of the sound-symbol correspondences, words, associated meanings, sentence structure, discourse structures and pragmatic aspects of their first language as well as some aspects of the new language they are learning. They have also built other schemata, equally important, which are based on their knowledge and experience of the world, including cultural values, beliefs, and ways of talking and interacting which are learned with their first language (Watson-Gegeo and Gegeo 1986).

Goodman (1977), Smith (1973), and many others have argued that the concepts which a reader brings to a text are actually more important than the text itself for comprehension (the construction of meaning). These are the concepts which are applied when the reader activates "top-down" processing strategies, as mentioned above. In comprehending, the textual material itself is "gobbledy-gook unless the reader can breathe meaning into it" (McNeil 1987; see also Kolers 1973; Smith 1977).

But when second language learners rely too heavily on top-down processing to comprehend a text, they can be misled if their interpretations are based on cultural schemata which do not match those the author had in mind. This was clearly shown in a study by Steffensen, Joag-dev and Anderson (1979). They gave the same reading passage to two groups, Indians from India and Americans in the United States.

> Each group read two passages, one about a typical American wedding and one about a typical Indian wedding. Subjects read what for them was the native passage more rapidly, recalled a larger amount of information from the native passage, produced more culturally appropriate elaborations of the native passage, and produced more culturally based distortions of the

foreign passage. Whether recalling the native or foreign passage, subjects recalled more text elements rated as important by other subjects with the same cultural heritage. These results show the pervasive influence of cultural schemata on comprehension and memory. (Reynolds et al 1982).

Clearly our cultural orientations and prior experiences influence our interpretations. To test this notion on yourself, read the passage which follows and decide what you think the author is describing.

At first you believe it is absolutely impossible to do, no matter how hard you concentrate. In fact, it always does take some time to get it right. Then, just when you get used to doing it competently, you hear of the alternate method. While the final choice is, of course, left to you, if you are mature and reasonable you'll realize that there is one way which is superior. People sometimes need to do it in strange positions, so flexibility is definitely an asset. Taken seriously, this task should not result in injuries. One usually tries to avoid situations where one has to do it too often.

(Zupnik 1988)

This was written as a description of learning to tie your shoelaces. But many other interpretations have been put forth, including changing the oil in your car, learning a new dance, and tying a bow tie.

Implications for Teachers

It is important for you to recognize that the reader brings something important to a text: previously acquired schemata — networks of prior interpretations (McNeill, 1987:6) — which are the basis for comprehending. The meaning of a text is constructed by the reader, who makes connections between the text and what is known about the world, based on the individual's cultural values, beliefs, native language discourse processes, and consciousness of language. (See vanDijk and Kintsch 1983:56.)

Therefore, the PROCESS shown in Diagram I may be universal, (as Goodman has posited, 1971), but THE RESULTING INTERPRETATION is cultural (D'Andrade 1981; van Dijk and Kintsch 1983; Nespor 1987; Stein 1986). In order for students to comprehend texts in standard English, they need to develop new schemata of language, text, and interpretation, as well as schemata of alternative cultural practices and values.

The Connection Between Reading and Literacy

If it is true that learning to read and comprehend a second language requires learning cultural interpretations, understanding cultural beliefs about language and discourse, and developing culture-specific formal and content schemata then reading and comprehending a new language means literally altering the learners' cognitive structures and value orientations. Teaching reading in standard English to second language learners and other limited English proficient students, then, can be seen as teaching an alternative cultural literacy.

WHAT IS LITERACY?

Many exciting advances have been made in our understanding of the nature and acquisition of literacy, thanks to work by such scholars as Besnier, Cole, Cook-Gumperz, deCastell, Gee, Graff, Heath, Luke, Olson, Ong, Pattison, Schieffelin, R. and S. Scollon, Scribner, Street, Wagner, and Watson-Gegeo. This section presents an overview of some current thinking about literacy as well as and some important implications of these ideas for English teachers (Gee 1986).

Until recently, literacy was viewed, quite simply, as the ability to decode and encode a language, in other words, the ability to recognize and pronounce sound-symbol correspondences and to produce the language in symbolic form. In fact, in the past that is all that was required in order to be considered literate.

Among many teachers of English as a second or foreign language, the term *literacy* is still often used that way. In second or foreign language programs, teaching literacy usually means introducing the concept of print to students who have no knowledge of printed language at all, or else it means teaching adults who, for some reason, have not developed basic reading and writing abilities.

But today literacy often means reading and writing in socially approved ways, at any age. Literacy is actually a very broad term. Decoding and encoding, important skills for the further development of literacy, might be termed "elementary literacy." The further development of literacy includes the acquisition of reading/thinking/interpreting skills as well as the ability to write (and speak) in forms which are recognized as standard English.

There is no argument with the necessity for teaching elementary literacy. The disagreement lies with certain common assumptions: a) that elementary literacy is all there is to literacy; and b) that such activities as learning the names and sounds of letters and words are disconnected from cultural values and beliefs. On the contrary, in learning the letter and sound-symbol correspondences in English, the student begins to develop new schemata of language. Elementary literacy — "learning your letters" — already contains cultural attitudes and values about language. For example, the type of orthography (ideographic or phonetic) a language employs is closely related to the way speakers of that language think. And, for another example, not all language groups consider it natural to learn the letters of their "alphabet" as we do our "a b c's" in English. It is important to remember that even teaching elementary literacy is teaching culture.

Recent research demonstrates that literacy is culturally defined and that it is more than the technical process of decoding and encoding (Cook-Gumperz 1986; Street 1984). According to many scholars, (Gee 1987; Heath 1983; Pattison 1982; Scollon and Scollon 1981; Watson-Gegeo and Gegeo 1986), literacy is more accurately defined as a set of attitudes about written language which develop within a cultural context. In every local culture, reading and writing are used to express, expand, and support cultural values. In any society, the tasks to be accomplished which require reading and writing greatly influence how literacy is defined. What counts as literacy is determined by what the dominant values are and by what the dominant culture deems to be appropriate ways of reading and writing and talking about text.*

---

* Throughout this book, the work *text* is meant to refer to any comprehensible printed matter, and is not limited to school textbooks.

The definition of literacy is cultural and depends on the time and place. For example, in the United States, prior to World War I, anyone who could decode and encode could probably carry out most written language tasks. But today, much more complex uses of reading and writing are demanded, and consequently the definition of basic literacy has changed to meet those demands. And so, when someone says that a recent high school graduate is functionally illiterate, they probably mean that the young person cannot accomplish with written language those tasks which our society regards as necessary today.

The Connections Between Language and Literacy

Attitudes toward reading and writing flow naturally out of the ways a local culture uses oral language (Heath 1983; Scollon and Scollon 1981; Watson-Gegeo and Gegeo 1986). Heath (1983), for example, reported in *Ways with Words* that in a rural Black American context, reading and writing were shared and interpreted in groups. To read alone was viewed as unusual at best and antisocial at worst. She found that in this population, *all* activities were group activities. Sense-making was a group effort, so it was not surprising that what she termed "literacy events" should also be group efforts. But in a nearby white American township, Heath found little evidence of group reading and interpreting. Instead, the emphasis was on getting the "truth" from a text, and it was not unusual for one person to read alone. This group valued the Bible and believed in literal truth.

Pattison (1982) has described a historical example of this. In ancient Greece, the Spartans and the Athenians both adopted writing and reading practices at about the same time. Yet these two cultures made very different uses of the printed word! These differences grew out of their already-established values and beliefs and their consciousness of language.

> Once introduced into Greece (Athens), writing soon enhanced the already existing predisposition of the Greeks to treat language with critical vigor and wit. (p. 52)
>
> But conditions were not right for the development of writing in all the Greek states . . . . . The Spartan reticence about the use of writing results from their general approach to language . . . . Education for the Spartan was only secondarily about language; foremost it was training in the habits of good citizenship . . . The Spartan ideal glorifies action and views language arts warily. (p. 56–57)

Cross cultural research indicates that varying attitudes toward the printed word are evident, and that these differences reflect differing attitudes about language in general. Here are several examples:

A. The way ideas are organized varies across cultures. Originally called to our attention by Kaplan (1966), this proposition has inspired contrastive research in several different languages. Ostler (1987:171) states that the structure of expository writing in a language "reflects the rhetorical patterns esteemed in their native cultures . . . . When individuals write other than their native language, they tend to use their native patterns in that discourse." Researchers have found that significant differences in text organization exist between English and Korean, German, Japanese (Eggington 1987; Hinds 1987), Arabic (Ostler 1987), and Athabaskan Eskimo (Scollon and Scollon 1981), to name a few.

According to Ostler (1987), modern classical Arabic embodies the values of parallel structure, balance, rhythmical coordination and symmetry found in the *Qu'ran*, which is based on oral language. In Arabic writing, all levels of language — from word choice to overall rhetorical pattern — exemplify these values. Arabic schools teach language and grammar through the *Qu'ran*, and this is done deliberately in order to maintain the sacred language.

In contrast, English-speaking writers value "variety of sentence structure and the use of subordination [of ideas] and deletion [of redundancies]" (Ostler 1987:172). So it is no wonder that speakers of Arabic often have difficulty learning to write and comprehend texts in English. This has been noted by Israeli English teachers when they teach reading comprehension to students from Semitic language backgrounds. Those students also find it difficult to learn to mark texts, skip words, or read critically (Zupnik 1988).

It is logical to conclude from this that when individuals *read* a second or foreign language, they comprehend best what meets their beliefs and expectations about the rhetorical patterns of written language. To the extent that these patterns are different from those of their first language, the language learner is likely to have difficulty comprehending (see Carrell 1984).

B. Cultures vary regarding their view of the role and responsibility of the reader and the writer.

Hinds (1987) states that "In Japan, perhaps in Korea, and certainly in Ancient China . . . . . it is the responsibility of the listener (or reader) to understand what it is that the speaker or author had intended to say" (p. 144). In contrast, he finds that "English speakers, by and large, charge the writer, or speaker, with the responsibility to make clear and well-organized statements" (p. 143).

In terms of reading, this means that in Japanese, Korean, or Chinese, a careful, word-by-word reading of a text may be necessary in order to ferret out the author's intended meaning. People from these language groups may not be able to recognize, at first, that reading in English does not require such careful, text-bound interpretation.

C. Narrative structure is not the same for every culture. The narrative usually has three parts in English, but in other languages, a story may be divided into four or five parts. (See Hymes 1981, especially chapters 3 and 4.)

Further, a narrative in standard English is expected to be topic centered, that is, to have one controlling topic, one central idea. All parts of the narrative are subordinated to that topic. In contrast, speakers of languages based on oral traditions, including Black English (Gee 1985) and Athabaskan Eskimo (Scollon and Scollon 1981), form narratives which are topic-associated. That is, many related topics can be included in one narrative. The associations are not usually made explicit, but the audience's awareness of their existence is assumed by the speaker or writer.

Eggington (1987:166) summarizes the implications of these ideas:

> If reading is to be considered a 'psycholinguistic guessing game,' as Goodman (1970:93) has posited, then readers and writers have certain built-in expectations about the ordering of ideas in any stretch of discourse. In an optimal condition, the reader shares the same expectations of what is to follow what as does the writer. Breakdowns in communication between writer and reader occur when these expectations are violated (Clyne 1980; Martin 1980).

Second language teachers often (consciously or unconsciously) expect reading skills from the first language to transfer to the second. The foregoing is important evidence for *not* expecting that to happen. Reading a language requires more than the mechanical decoding of print — it requires knowledge of particular ways of thinking and talking about print — not only recognizing words and sentences, but recognizing culturally-based forms and making culturally-favored interpretations.

Literacy Acquisition and Reading — Implications for Teaching

Because every language has a different way of making sense of the world, learning to comprehend written text in a second or foreign language is a complex task. Anthropologists and linguists have shown what an important role culture plays in this enterprise.

What this means for reading instruction is that English teachers can no longer ignore the social context in which reading is taught and learned. In the United States, in schools, reading is not a simple, value-free technology which teachers can pass on to their students. Reading well in English means being able to interpret a text in ways which are expected by "mainstream" culture.

Heath (1984) made an important distinction between literacy skills and literate skills. *Literacy skills*, she stated, are the decoding and encoding skills, while *literate skills* are the thinking processes about reading and writing which are influenced by the culture. In teaching reading, instructors need to be involved in helping language learners acquire the literate skills which will aid them in comprehending texts in standard English.

Heath pointed out that in order to comprehend texts in English, the reader must learn to treat language as an object in and of itself, be comfortable with anaylzing things (taking the text apart), and make connections between what a text is about and external, absent objects, ideas, and people. Hoffman and Heath (1984) noted that facility with the essay-text language style prevalent in schools, universities, and businesses in the United States requires a person to be able to use language to:

- talk about an on-going sequence of events
- compare one phenomenon or text with another
- explain causes and effects
- render near-verbatim re-tellings
- tell stories
- experience print as a source of new information
- examine ideas from multiple points of view

Many children learn these literate skills before they even begin school, because they use similar language practices at home. (Heath 1983; Schieffelin and Cochran-Smith 1984). These children are said to come from "mainstream" families, that is, families whose ways of talking to each other include the features listed above. But students who do not grow up with this kind of language experience have difficulty with school literacy. This is true of non-mainstream native speakers of English as well as ESL/EFL students.

Heath (1984:25) argued that many ESL/EFL students have not been socialized into ways of talking and thinking which are the basis of academic language. "For most of our students," she wrote, "we have to make explicit the academic habits of using oral and written language which the school requires, and we have to provide social interactive meaningful occasions for repeating these habits again and again."

"Mainstream" or school literacy reflects specific learned attitudes about language. One can conclude that it is how one *thinks and talks* about the text that matters. That is the cultural part of reading which second language students must learn.

You can teach your students the skills needed for effective reading by employing a methodology that focuses on the cognitive processes and language practices which are the basis of literate behavior in English. In fact, it is the teacher's responsibility to ensure that second language and other "non-mainstream" students learn these literate skills. Gee (1986) has argued:

> Short of radical social change, there is no access to power in the society without control over the discourse practices in thought, speech, and writing of essay-text literacy.

However, it should be understood that what is being taught is not an inherently better, value-free approach to comprehending text. It is teaching another way of thinking about language, an alternative way of interpreting text, a different consciousness, complete with values and attitudes which are likely to be at odds with the students' own. For example, students who have learned how to tell stories at home may have a different format for story-telling than what is found in literate texts (Michaels 1986). We can teach the basic story forms found in English texts in ways that allow our students to retain their own cultural story forms. (See also Kintsch 1977.)

Consequently, English teachers should be aware of the fact that "values are an inherent part of reading comprehension" (Stein 1986:179). Teaching reading may turn out to be teaching an alternative way of thinking and talking about text, a way required for academic success in English. But it is not the *only correct way*. It is important that students retain respect for their own cultural ways with words.

WHAT STUDENTS NEED TO BE ABLE TO DO TO READ EFFECTIVELY

1. They need to develop new schemata about what reading is and how it is done effectively in English.
2. They need to break the habit of reading every word.
3. They need to learn how to tap their background knowledge in order to better employ top-down processing.
4. They need to acquire some of the skills which fluent readers of English employ unconsciously in order to strengthen their bottom-up processing abilities.
5. They need to acquire those reading skills which will enhance the interaction of top-down and bottom-up processing modes.
6. They need to learn to be able to read faster.
7. They need to learn to read in English for pleasure.

TEACHING READING: APPLYING RESEARCH TO PRACTICE

Based on the above, we can conclude that second language students need to learn to think in English in order to read effectively in English. Before discussing a specific methodology for teaching reading, we will consider, very briefly, the conclusions and recommendations of educational researchers.

- Cognitive pscyhologists have shown in their research that students learn new strategies or thinking processes most effectively when they are consciously aware that they are doing so (Brown, Armbruster and Baker, 1986). Once they are conscious of the processes, students can monitor their comprehension and apply appropriate strategies as needed for comprehending a text (Brown 1978).

  Interacting and talking about text in particular ways is essential (Casanave 1988). In addition, Heath (1984, 1986), Vygotsky (1962), and others have found that students develop literate skills when teachers encourage them to talk about written language, when teachers model comprehension strategies for them, and when students have opportunities to talk to each other about how they make sense of a text.

- Eskey (1986) has stated that second language students must learn to read faster if they wish to improve their reading in English.

- Krashen (1985) has posited that the best way to improve reading is by reading. His survey of methodologies led him to conclude that simply allowing students to read more books will result in improved reading just as often, if not more often, than any instructional program.

Putting this all together, it is clear that students will learn to read in English best in a class which includes, on a regular basis, the following components:

1. Substantial opportunities for reading self-selected books for pleasure and for talking about their books with persons who can model literate skills.

2. Focused, interactive lessons on specific reading skills, with opportunities to apply the skills to a variety of texts.

3. Training and practice in speeded reading.

PART II Pleasure Reading

Pleasure reading is introduced early in this book to make a point: On-going immersion in extensive reading is essential for developing and applying all of the specific reading skills (Eskey 1986). The position taken here is that students must develop the habit of reading massive amounts in English. Research shows that vocabulary acquisition and writing ability are directly related to the quantity of reading students engage in (Krashen 1985). (Also see Nuttall 1982 for additional information about pleasure reading.)

SELF-SELECTED BOOKS FOR PLEASURE READING

As Edelsky remarked (1986:171), many so-called literacy events in school, where printed text is present, are not authentic reading or writing activities because language is not being used in its fullest sense. Often, for example, the readers or other teacher-selected texts used in second or foreign language classrooms are inauthentic, because the students (and often the teacher) are really not interested in the information found in the text. The students can see that the only reason for reading the text is because it is a language lesson, not because of a transfer of knowledge or information through the medium of print. As students and teachers know, the only place where you read readers is in school.

This is not to argue that there is no role for readers! They are valuable for providing a structured sequence of language-based instruction, and they can often serve as a source for intensive reading lessons (for applying reading skills which students have already learned). But let us agree that readers are not appropriate for pleasure reading.

For pleasure reading, students should read self-selected books (Krashen 1985). There are a number of pedagogical and psychological reasons for this:

First, students' language weaknesses can be balanced by background knowledge about the topics of the books they select. Students tend to select books on subjects which they already know something about. Their familiarity with the topic and/or the genre can enable them to read books which might otherwise be too difficult (linguistically). As they read, they can grow aware of the fact that they are able to guess word meanings because of their knowledge of the subject.

Second, students' motivation for reading increases when they read what they are interested in. Since reading improves with practice, reading self-selected books should consequently lead to improved reading.

Third, self-selected books are authentic reading materials. Writers of traditional ESL/EFL readers maintain that they present "authentic" readings in their books, but a text is not authentic unless there is a genuine information gap and the text is being read in order to gain information or pleasure. Assigned texts in other school situations are different; they are part of a course on a specific subject. But ESL/EFL readers are not usually part of a course on any subject. They offer *practice* for the real thing. Students should *have* the real thing in reading classes.

Finally, selecting their own book is an important aspect of literate behavior which may be new to some students. We want them to learn that there is something special about selecting and reading a book. That feeling does not occur when the same text is part of a reader. This is a cultural attitude, and a very important one to develop, particularly if students are from cultures which foster very different attitudes about books. Approaching, handling, examining books; comparing, choosing, and talking about books are all part of building new schemata for literate behavior.

WHAT SHOULD STUDENTS READ?

Students should read whole books by a single author, not magazines or collections of short stories by a variety of authors. This allows the student to develop a print "relationship" with a single native speaker: the author. The vocabulary range will be limited by the topic of the book and the author's finite lexicon, and once a student "gets into" a book, the author's style, sentence structures, and viewpoint will become familiar, and the student's reading fluency will increase.

Reading Levels

Beginners. Several series of books have been written or adapted especially for beginning level ESL/EFL students. These include the Newbury House Readers, the Regents Readers, Longman's American Structural Readers, Longman's Simplified Readers, and Oxford's Progressive English Readers.

Another source for beginning level books are publishers' series for Adult Basic Education, such as the Jamestown Adult Learners Series and the Scott, Foresman Adult Readers Library. Other publishers of Adult Basic Education materials have also produced books for pleasure reading, but in many cases the linguistic structures, idioms, and other assumptions about cultural knowledge make them unsuitable for many students.

High beginners and up. As soon as students have achieved reading comprehension levels of about United States grade four, they can read books which were *not* especially adapted for limited English proficient students. One good source of pleasure reading books is the young adult section of the local bookstore or public library. In the past 20 years, there has been a remarkable increase in the number and quality of "easy reading," high-interest books written especially for young adults. Most students, even mature adults, can find a book which appeals to them from the wide range available.

Intermediate and up. Many books are accessible to students at this level: Both fiction and non-fiction books which were written for native speakers.

Suggested Books

This list was compiled from the selection available at a large local bookstore, from publishers' catalogs, and from former students' recommendations.

Although students should be encouraged to read whatever interests them, most of the books on this list are fiction. Because the range of interests of second language students is very broad, any list of non-fiction books would very likely be off target. Furthermore, experience has shown that many students refuse to read fiction because they do not consider it "serious reading." These students should be encouraged to read at least one book of fiction, because otherwise this gap in their reading experience will prevent them from learning about the benefits of reading fiction, including the immersion in a source of natural, informal English as it is used by native speakers.

The books listed here were selected on the basis of these criteria:

1. Are they interesting to read? Will they appeal to a student who is learning English as a second or foreign language?

2. Is the language relatively straightforward and accessible? Is the book free of regional dialect, wordy, page-long paragraphs, and obscure, five-syllable words? (In other words, we will have to put Twain and Dickens on hold for a while.)

3. Is the theme more or less universal? Does the book require only a minimum of cultural background knowledge to "get the story"?

These books are suitable for students who are 12 years old and up. Starred selections indicate that the author has written other good books of the same type for the same audience. Many of these books were originally intended for children or young adults. The children's books are classics which will add to the students' store of cultural information; the young adult books usually deal with contemporary issues in straightforward language. As always, teacher discretion is advised.

Low Intermediate and Up

Lloyd Alexander	The Black Cauldron*
Maya Angelou	I Know Why the Caged Bird Sings
Avi	Sometimes I Think I Hear My Name
James Baldwin	If Beale Street Could Talk
John Baskin	New Burlington: The Life and Death of an American Village
Jay Bennett	Deathman, Do Not Follow Me*
Judy Blume	Forever*
Joe David Brown	Paper Moon
Sheila Burnford	The Incredible Journey
John Cristopher	The White Mountains
Vera and Bill Cleaver	Me, Too*
James L. Collier and Christopher Collier	My Brother Sam Is Dead*
Robert Cormier	The Chocolate War*
Lois Duncan	Killing Mr. Griffin*
Esther Forbes	Johnny Tremain
Ernest J. Gaines	The Autobiography of Miss Jane Pitman
Jean George	My Side of the Mountain
William Gibson	The Miracle Worker (a play)
Bette Green	The Summer of My German Soldier
Rosa Guy	Friends
Nat Hentoff	Jazz Country*

S. E. Hinton	That Was Then, This Is Now*
Isabel Holland	Hitchhike
Jean and James Houston	Farewell to Manzanar
M. E. Kerr	Dinky Hocker Shoots Smack*
Norma Klein	Sunshine*
Joanna Lee	I Want to Keep My Baby
Ursula K. LeGuin	Very Far Away From Anywhere Else
Madeleine L'Engle	A Wrinkle In Time*
Lucy Maud Montgomery	Anne of Green Gables
Farley Mowatt	The Dog Who Wouldn't Be
John Neufeld	Edgar Allen*
Scott O'Dell	The Black Pearl*
Richard Peck	Are You In the House Alone?
Marjorie Kinnan Rawlings	The Yearling
Johanna Reiss	The Upstairs Room
W. H. D. Rouse	Gods, Heroes, and Men of Ancient Rome
Anne Snyder	My Name is Davy — I'm an Alcoholic
John Steinbeck	The Pearl
E. B. White	Charlotte's Web*
Laura Ingalls Wilder	Little House on the Prairie*
Paul Zindel	The Pigman*

High Intermediate and Up

Louisa May Alcott	Little Women
Anonymous	Go Ask Alice
Jean Auel	The Clan of the Cave Bear*
Charlotte Bronte	Jane Eyre
James Carroll	Madonna Red*
Willa Cather	Death Comes to the Archbishop
Kate Chopin	The Awakening
Mary Higgins Clark	Where Are the Children?*
Robin Cook	Coma*
James Gould Cozzens	S. S. San Pedro
Howard Fast	Freedom Road
John Hersey	Hiroshima
James Hilton	Good-bye, Mr. Chips
Lee Iacocca	Iacocca
Daniel Keyes	Flowers for Algernon
Marie Killilea	Karen
Jerzy Kosinski	Being There

Jack London	The Call of the Wild
Alistair Maclean	San Andreas*
Christopher Morley	Parnassus on Wheels
Tim O'Brien	If I Die in a Combat Zone
George Orwell	Animal Farm
Ayn Rand	Anthem
Elizabeth G. Speare	The Witch of Blackbird Pond
Danielle Steele	The Promise*
John Steinbeck	The Red Pony*
Theodore Taylor	HMS Hood vs. Bismarck
Carrie Ten Boom	The Hiding Place
Anne Tyler	Dinner At the Homesick Restaurant*
Elie Weisel	Night*

Notes

1. See also *A World of Books — An Annotated Reading List for ESL/EFL Students*, Second Edition, Revised, by Dorothy S. Brown.

2. Research has indicated (Sivell 1987) that some students, when given a choice, select books which are much too easy for them. They should be encouraged to try the more difficult books. Conversely, some students select books which are much too difficult, perhaps because they do not understand that they are supposed to read for PLEASURE. They may be trying to impress the teacher (and maybe themselves) by selecting books which are far beyond their comprehension abilities. Such difficult texts will discourage them, and they won't want to read at all. It is best if students are carefully led to books which are within their grasp.

3. Students are usually pretty evenly split between fiction and non-fiction when they select books. No matter which they read, their reading can serve to facilitate the development of literate behaviors. According to Heath (1984), ESL/EFL students need to experience the enculturation to essay-text literacy experienced by many native speakers. So *what* students read is not as important as the fact that they *read* the books and then *discuss* their reading as an "apprentice" with a more literate native speaker.

4. Teachers sometimes wonder what to do about students who feel limited by the unfamiliar vocabulary they encounter when they read for pleasure. Should they stop at each unknown word and look it up? Stopping to look up every new word interrupts the flow of reading. We want students to read fast enough to be able to follow the story or understand the ideas presented in their books.

   An approach that seems to work is to instruct students to guess at unknown words, and if they cannot understand the text by guessing, they should use the dictionary as a last resort. But they should limit their use of the dictionary to no more than five words per page of text. If they need to use the dictionary any more than that, they are probably reading a book that is too difficult for them.

WHEN SHOULD STUDENTS READ FOR PLEASURE?

In Class. Class time can be regularly scheduled for silent reading. Many students have never developed the habit of just sitting still and reading. When class time is set aside for pleasure reading, students recognize that you consider it a meaningful activity and they begin to take it more seriously. If you plan at least 15 minutes for pleasure reading and join in to read a book, too, especially early in the semester, students will have a role model for silent reading. In many schools, Sustained Silent Reading (SSR) is a regular occurrence. Teachers, students, custodians, office staff, and administrators all stop to read their own books for 15–20 minutes every day. (See Krashen 1985 for a summary of research on SSR.)

At Home. If possible, pleasure reading should be the only homework assignment from the reading class, and students should be instructed to read for at least 30 minutes every day. But developing the habit of daily reading is not easy — students need help in the form of motivating techniques and monitoring.

1. Students can use a graph to keep a record of their reading: date, number of pages read, and time. A graph can also be used for working on increasing reading rate with the student's book. (See page 59.)

   (Directions for calculating words per page appear on page 58. Students should learn to do the calculations for themselves.)

2. Students can be required to bring their books and graphs to class every day, and you can check the graph to see how much progress they have made. This checking can be done in just a couple of minutes if the students place their graphs on their desks while you walk around and glance at them, making appropriate comments as needed.

3. Once a week, you can ask if anyone in the class has completed a book. A few words of praise for those who have can be a powerful incentive to others. The students who have finished books can answer a few gently-posed questions about the author, title, genre, and length of their books, as well as their opinions of the books.

4. Another informal method can also be used to ensure that students read regularly. You can take a couple of minutes at the beginning of class once a week to ask each student what page they are on in their book and how many pages they read the night before. You can do this in a friendly, teasing way, and yet exert pressure on the students. Of course, your judgement is vital in deciding if this is an appropriate technique for your class.

MAKING BOOKS AVAILABLE FOR STUDENTS

Being surrounded by a print environment is essential (Krashen 1985). If the reading classroom has a library of books for the students to choose from, this immediate availability will allow you to guide students to books at the appropriate level of difficulty. The books can be arranged on shelves labeled according to level of difficulty, and within the levels, by type of book: fiction (mystery, romance, science fiction, fantasy, intrigue), and non-fiction (by subject). The arrangement itself is a lesson: students learn about the categories of books as they browse among them. (See Bamford 1984; Nuttall 1982.)

It may be difficult to imagine starting a classroom library when not a single book is available. One way to begin is to ask friends, relatives, and other teachers to contribute books they no longer need. Students, too, can be encouraged to buy books and to donate them to the class library after they have finished reading them. In some cities, the public library has book sales which offer used library paperback books for less than one dollar. A school budget might include several dollars a year for books. After a few semesters, the number of books in the class library seems to increase willy-nilly.

In addition, the class routine can include periodic trips to local book shops and libraries. Such outings emphasize the importance of browsing and allow the students to become acquainted with the wide variety of books available.

BOOK CONFERENCES

You may be reluctant to allow students to read individually selected books because you may feel that it would be impossible to monitor the students' reading. When all the students in the class read the same book, you may feel a sense of control because it is quite a simple matter to test the students' understanding of the book.

Some teachers assign written book reports as a means of keeping the students accountable for their pleasure reading. But writing book reports can actually discourage many students from reading, because writing in a second language is a very difficult task. In fact, the written book report turns pleasure reading into a writing assignment.

A very pleasant and productive way to deal with this situation is to hold individual book conferences with students after they have finished reading their individually selected books. However, the book conference should not be viewed as a time for questions to find out if the student comprehended the book (and definitely not the time for a quiz). In fact, you should not even take notes which might appear to be an evaluation. The student *should* see you "check off" his or her name, perhaps with a date, to ensure that the student realizes that the book conference, even though informal, really "counts" as school work.

The book conference is an opportunity for you to model a native speaker's way of discussing books. In a one-on-one conversation with each student about the book they have read, you can demonstrate the cultural attitudes toward print which many native speakers take for granted as "natural." In fact, we are all socialized into cultural ways of discussing books, and you can provide the "scaffolding" for the student who is learning a new way to interact with text. By carefully including a variety of elaborative questions in the book conference, you can raise the student's awareness of this approach. Remember to control the level of difficulty of the questions during the book conference, beginning with only a few in mind.

Elaborative Question types:

Expressive (How did you like the book?)

Factual (Who is the main character? Where is the story set?)

Informational (What was it about?)

Experiential (Did anything like that ever happen to you?)

Affective (How did that make you feel?)

Relational (Did you ever hear of anything like this in your country?)

Critical (Do you think this could really happen?)

Predictive (What do you think will happen next?)

Stylistic (Did you think the author did a good job in making that character seem real?)

Sequential (What happened after that?)

Cause/Effect (What made the tree fall into the road?)

Summarizing (Can you tell the whole story in just a few sentences?)

Speculative (What would this story be like if the nurse was telling the story instead of the doctor?)

Inferential (Why do you think the family waited so long before taking the baby to the doctor?)

Obviously you will not ask all of these types of questions at every conference. The format of a book conference is conversational, and informality is essential. After two or three questions, the discussion will take on a life of its own, and you may find that many of the elaborative questions arise naturally in the course of the conversation.

Logistics

A common objection to the idea of book conferences is that a teacher cannot possibly read "all those books!" But book conferences do not require that. Indeed, it is good if you have *not* read the books! In school, the student is rarely the knowledgable participant in the exchange of information. A book conference offers an opportunity for the student to play that role. The students' and the teacher's awareness of this information gap in the book conference empowers students, encourages them to take risks, and keeps them talking!

A practical objection to book conferences is the time factor. How can you find the time to spend anywhere from 15 to 30 minutes with each student several times during the term? This requires some juggling, and the solution will be local, depending on the type of program and the space available.

One way is to take one student out of the class for a book conference during the class pleasure reading time. Another way is to make appointments just before or just after class, or during your office hours, if they are part of the program schedule. It is sometimes feasible to take one student out of class for a book conference while the rest of the students are working on reading skills lessons in pairs or small groups.

Benefits of Book Conferences

The benefits of book conferences far outweigh their logistical difficulty. Besides the opportunity for students to learn new ways of thinking about and discussing books, there are these possible outcomes:

1. The teacher and the student get to know each other better. Teachers have reported that their conferences with some of their quiet students caused them to revise their estimation of the students' abilities.

2. The student has the opportunity to relate school reading to his/her own life and past experience.

3. The teacher can suggest other books which the student might enjoy.

4. The student might suggest some other books which the teacher might enjoy!

5. The student speaks in English about something on which he/she is the expert, and for second language learners, that is highly motivating.

6. The conference gives the reading of books an important status and encourages students to read more.

7. Shy students who do not like to speak in front of the class have a chance to speak.

8. Students have an occasion to speak their mind. Quite often, the conversation strays off the actual topic of the book, and students are able to express feelings about important, sometimes personal, issues.

9. Students from cultures which do not encourage reading alone, but rather encourage group interpretation, will have the opportunity to display skills in interactive interpretation in which they may excel.

10. Students love these conferences!

Peer Conferences

If the goal is to give the students a maximum number of opportunities to talk about their reading in literate ways, two or three book conferences with you can help. But certainly the students can benefit from more practice. Besides, students should have a chance to play both roles in the book conference, not only responding to but also generating questions. Peer conferences can provide these opportunities. (See Manning and Manning 1984, cited in Krashen 1985.)

It is important that students learn to ask elaborative questions in a peer conference. However, it would be inappropriate for you to provide a list of written questions for peer work, because the conference would be teacher-centered and it might seem to be a test. Besides, one of the objectives of the peer conference is to give the students opportunities to learn to ask literate questions.

There are several methods of training the students so that peer conferences will result in literate discussions of books.

1. Early in the semester, you can present a lesson to the whole class, using a tape recording or a video tape of a model book conference. (For example, as a part of a literacy project in a California elementary school, Heath produced a video tape called "Inside Learners" [Hoffman and Heath 1986], which shows fifth-grade girls reading books to first-graders and asking them elaborative questions.) You can instruct the students to take note of the kinds of questions that come up during the model conference. The students can be allowed to review the tape as many times as necessary in order to write down some of the questions they would like to use.

2. The students can tape and then listen to and analyze their book conferences with you, once again taking note of the types of questions you asked.

3. Students can tape record their peer conferences and then analyze the discussion in order to find out what kinds of questions they asked, and what they wish that they had included in the conference. (These tapes should be guaranteed "private and confidential.") Students can report the results of their analysis orally to you or to the whole class, or in writing. In either case, the language will be about the literate skills which they are developing.

OTHER FEEDBACK ABOUT THE BOOKS

Another way for students to let each other know their thoughts and feelings about their books is via a Book Response Form. The form below has been used in an intensive English program with students aged 16–50.

BOOK RESPONSE SHEET

Title of book _____

Author _____

Type of book _____

Number of pages _____

Level of difficulty for you: Easy   Average   Difficult
What did you like best about this book?

What did you dislike about this book?

Would you tell a friend to read this book? Why?

Your language _____ Your country _____

Your age _____ Male or female? _____

Today's date _____

Such forms, of course, should not be graded or corrected in any way, nor should they be completed in conjunction with the book conference. They are useful for deciding which books to recommend to other students, and other students can refer to them when they are trying to find a good book to read. The completed forms should be available in the classroom for students to browse through.

The forms also serve as an additional lesson for the students. As they fill them in, students learn to think objectively about their books, and this practice will help them to write book reviews when they are assigned.

Conclusion

Reading for pleasure can transform a class into a book-centered, dynamic place. The students will read more, and they will acquire many of the cultural attitudes and values about books which are essential to developing literate skills. When pleasure reading is the final item on the class agenda, it is not uncommon, at the end of the hour, for students to say, "I can't leave yet . . . . I just have a few more pages to read."

PART III Teaching Reading Skills

This part of the book contains a detailed description of selected reading skills and an explanation of an approach for teaching the skills. This approach is effective for students who have already learned "elementary" literacy skills. The sample exercises included here are at several levels of linguistic difficulty.

A. BACKGROUND, RATIONALE, AND METHODOLOGY

What are Reading Skills?

The reading skills listed below foster the thinking processes which students need to develop in order to read standard English effectively. The list is not exhaustive, and the skills, some of which overlap, will be familiar to many teachers.

Reading Skills

1. Automatic decoding. Being able to recognize a word at a glance.
2. Previewing and Predicting. Giving the text a quick once-over to be able to guess what is to come.
3. Specifying purpose. Knowing why a text is being read.
4. Identifying genre. Knowing the nature of the text in order to predict what the form and content will be.
5. Questioning. Asking questions in an inner dialog with the author.
6. Scanning. Looking through a text very rapidly for specific information.
7. Recognizing topics. Finding out what the text is about.
8. Classification of ideas into main topics and details. Categorizing words and ideas on the basis of their relationships; distinguishing general and specific.
9. Locating topic sentences. Identifying, where possible, the sentence in a passage which is the generalization.
10. Stating the main idea of a sentence, paragraph or passage. Knowing what the author is expressing about the topic.
11. Recognizing patterns of relationships. Identifying the relationships between ideas; the overall structure of the text.
12. Identifying and using words which signal the patterns of relationships. Being able to see connections between ideas by the use of words such as *first, then, later*.
13. Inferring the main idea, using patterns and other clues.
14. Recognizing and using pronouns, referents, and other lexical equivalents as clues to cohesion.
15. Guessing the meaning of unknown words from the context. Using such clues as knowledge of word parts, syntax, and relationship patterns.
16. Skimming. Quickly getting the gist or overview of a passage or book.
17. Paraphrasing. Re-stating texts in the reader's own words in order to monitor one's own comprehension.

18. Summarizing. Shortening material by retaining and re-stating main ideas and leaving out details.

19. Drawing conclusions. Putting together information from several parts of the text and inducing new or additional ideas.

20. Drawing inferences and using evidence. Reading between the lines; using evidence in the text to know things that are unstated.

21. Visualizing. Picturing, or actually drawing a picture or diagram, of what is described in the text.

22. Reading critically. Judging the accuracy of a passage with respect to what the reader already knows; distinguishing fact from opinion.

23. Reading faster. Reading fast enough to allow the brain to process the input.

24. Adjusting reading rate according to materials and purpose. Being able to choose speed and strategies needed for the level of comprehension desired by the reader.

These skills are not new; most are familiar to anyone who has taught reading (or writing). But the approach taken in teaching them can make a dramatic difference. In addition to including practice on several of these skills in every reading lesson, as is common practice, *single* skills can be presented as units of instruction, with each skill as the focus of a series of lessons.

For instructional planning, it is useful to recognize that some skills enhance the "top-down" mode, some develop the "bottom-up" mode, and others enhance the interaction of the two. The sample exercises in this book have been grouped in this fashion. It should be clear that in reality the reader *never totally* employs only one mode of processing. Top-down and bottom-up modes are employed simultaneously.

But researchers have found that second language proficiency and background knowledge about the topic of a text are two factors which influence which mode the reader relies on most heavily when reading. As one would imagine, and as Coady's model (1979:8) illustrates, the less linguistic ability the reader has, the more the individual will be concerned with the elements of the text, looking for graphic clues which might trigger *some* level of comprehension (Bottom-up). On the other hand, those who are fluent in a language can use much more of their processing time in making connections between the text and what is already known (Top-down). (See also Stanovich 1982.)

Focusing on Specific Skills

There has been some disagreement among reading specialists about the value of breaking reading down into subskills and then working on them individually. Some reading professionals have argued that reading is a whole skill, impossible to break down (R. Thorndike 1974). However, research has shown that it is possible to divide reading into a series of subprocesses (Collins and Smith 1980; Schank and Abelson 1977).

It has also been argued that instruction on specific reading skills (subprocesses) does not transfer to other situations. However, that idea, too, has been contradicted by research such as that by Palinscar and Brown (1982). They showed that students can be trained in specific reading comprehension skills in a way that will enable them to transfer these skills to new reading situations.

In discussing that research, Brown, Armbruster, and Baker (1986:72) point out that:

Some possible reasons for the success of the Palinscar and Brown studies include:

1. Training was extensive. Students received approximately 20 days of instruction.

2. The trained activities were well specified theoretically and well established empirically as particular problems for poor readers.

3. The training was tailored to the needs of these students (good decoders but passive comprehenders).

4. The skills could be expected to be transsituational . . . . .

5. A great deal of attention was paid to "metacognitive" variables: students were informed of the importance, generality and utility of the activities . . . .

6. The reciprocal teaching mode permitted extensive [teacher] modeling in a reasonably natural setting, and forced the students to participate so teachers could evaluate current states and provide appropriate feedback and assistance.

7. Every attempt was made to increase the students' sense of personal efficacy; they plotted success, planned strategies, monitored progress, and were shown to be competent and *in control*.

Although Palinscar and Brown were working with first language readers, their principles can be applied to reading in a second language as well. In fact, their approach is very similar to the one we use throughout this book. As Hudson has remarked,

> It may be that the process of learning to read a second language is partially a matter of first experiencing skills and strategies as usable, and then abstracting principles for successful reading (1982:20).

Reading Skills as the Basis of Lessons

Many educators would agree that what students do during a class is what they learn. So, for example, in ESL/EFL classes where reading is taught using a content-based approach, students work on selections from readers which include lessons on several reading skills (as well as grammar, vocabulary, discussion, and writing exercises). Rarely are reading skills the *focus* — the lessons are about the language of the passage. Alderson and Urquart asserted that

> Such a pedagogic practice — of focusing on the language of a text — may be justified as a language lesson, but it may very well be counterproductive as a *reading* lesson (1984:246).

When students read a story and then discuss its content, or when they learn the vocabulary or grammatical structures found in a story, they may practice those reading skills which they already know, but it is very unlikely that they will learn new ones. After a reading class, students can say, "Today's lesson was about earthquakes (or fast food restaurants, or dating practices of American teenagers)," or they can say, "Today we learned how to preview (or how to decide how fast to read a passage, or how to identify the organization of an essay)." This is really a question of product versus process.

Obviously, it does not have to be one extreme or the other. But it can be argued that while content is a familiar focus in a language class, reading processes and consciousness of processes, are often new ideas for many students of English. They may not be accustomed to thinking that way. Furthermore, although the *teacher* may be conscious of both the content and the process involved in a lesson, it is not necessarily the case that the *students* will possess this awareness, *unless it is made explicit.*

Ironically, many ESL/EFL teachers have worked hard to design lessons which allow language learning to flow from the content of their lessons without the students' conscious awareness that they are actually doing, for example, a lesson on the present progressive tense verb forms. But for teaching reading/thinking skills, the opposite approach must be taken: the process of comprehending should be the explicit object of the lesson. Of course, the ability to read and understand a text through the automatic application of the skills is the objective. But skill-instruction highlights the analytical thinking processes to use in understanding a text in English.

Cognition and Metacognition

Since the late 1970s, cognitive skills and metacognition have been a major focus of research in cognitive psychology (Flavell and Wellman 1977; Meyer 1975). *Cognitive skills* are the strategies which the reader employs in making sense of a passage; the reading skills listed above are examples of cognitive skills. Research, mostly with first language speakers, has shown that students of all ages learn new strategies or thinking processes best when they are consciously aware of what they are doing and what their purpose is for doing it (Brown, Armbruster, and Baker 1986:74).

This means that reading skills lessons should not be taught as ''recipes'' or as rote exercises. Students should know the rationale for what they are learning and doing. According to Brown, Armbruster, and Baker (1986:68):

> Providing the rationale for each component strategy leads to an understanding of the significance of those activities, and this awareness contributes to continued unprompted use.

In other words, once they are conscious of the skills and how to use them, students can learn to monitor their own comprehension and apply appropriate strategies as needed for making sense of a text. And that is what is meant by *metacognition.*

According to McNeil (1987:91):

> Metacognition transcends cognition by enabling individuals not just to use particular strategies, but to be aware of the importance of these strategies and how to appraise them. Metacognition emphasizes broad control processes rather than highly specific task strategies.

McNeil (1987:92) describes three types of metacognitive processes:

- Self-knowledge — knowing one's own reading strengths and weaknesses;
- Task knowledge — knowing which strategies to use in a given situation;
- Self-monitoring — being aware of when one does not understand and knowing which strategies to use to deal with it (i.e., re-reading or reading ahead).

As students work on reading skills lessons, they can develop these three aspects of metacognition if they have opportunities to interact while they learn (Casanave 1988). As specific skills are mastered, intensive reading lessons (using selections from a reader, a newspaper, or a magazine) can provide additional practice in applying the reading skills, monitoring comprehension, and deciding what to do when comprehension breaks down. Once students have learned to use specific skills, they can learn to decide which ones to apply to make sense of a passage.

Teaching Interactive, Skill-Focused Lessons

A list of reading skills is not going to make a difference in and of itself. It is in the *approach to teaching the skills* that the "magic" occurs: students' discussing and consciously working on the skills promotes the cognitive and metacognitive behavior necessary for the development of effective reading.

When you design skill-focused reading comprehension lessons for your class, begin by deciding which reading skills would benefit your students the most. Often, the order in which the skills are listed on pages 25–26 proves effective. For each skill, it is a good idea to select or design a sequence of exercises which begins with very simple tasks and then gradually increases in complexity (Tierney and Cunningham 1984:640). As in the teaching of other language skills, it is important to remember that when a reading/thinking skill is the focus of the lesson, that skill should be the *only* challenge. The inclusion of new vocabulary items, unfamiliar concepts, or difficult grammatical structures in the same lesson usually clouds the issue and overloads the students.

Analyzing a text may be new to many students, especially ESL/EFL students. It is important to remember that the students will be more able to read (or write) in new ways if they have first learned to speak in new ways (Hoffman and Heath, 1986). Thus, a reading skill lesson should begin by providing opportunities for students to learn to use analytical language orally. The more the students talk, the more they will learn. Then they can apply these new ways of thinking and talking to their reading and writing. (These ideas are based on an understanding of learning developed by L. S. Vygotsky, whose work is cited in the bibliography.) In fact, outrageous as this may seem, beginners could be allowed to do the reading skill problem-solving in their own language, if necessary, in order to facilitate the development of the desired cognitive processes.

In addition, students need opportunities to develop a consciousness of themselves as readers in English. Methods for accomplishing this include teaching them to monitor their own progress, using a variety of record-keeping techniques, such as graphs, charts, and lists of books read. These devices also serve as motivating factors, and students usually gain a sense of satisfaction by looking back over the record of their efforts and accomplishments.

In the following section of this book, the sample lessons demonstrate a skill-focused approach to teaching reading, which is applicable at all levels of literacy. However, most of the sample exercises are meant for students who have already learned "elementary literacy." The reader will notice that the lessons usually involve as much speaking, writing, and listening as they do silent reading. There is metalinguistic activity in a reading class which takes this approach; the students think and talk about English as an object. There is metacognitive activity, as well, as students learn to talk and to think about their own thinking. The goal of the lessons is to encourage the students to be active, thinking readers.

Working in Pairs and Small Groups

In order to become aware of their own reading/thinking processes, it is essential that the students work in pairs or small groups when they work on most of the reading skills lessons. Such peer interaction can add interest and fun to the exercises as well as increase learning. (See Pica, Young, and Doughty 1987; Tierney and Cunningham 1984:640.)

It is not always easy to convince students to work together. For some, it may seem a bit like cheating. For others, there is an assumption that all learning comes from the teacher, and that listening to each other is a waste of time. And, occasionally, the students may come from cultures or nations between which a long history of animosity has existed. It is a real challenge to figure out how to get such students to work together. In fact, your sensitivity to these factors is a key element in making such collaborative learning work.

Of course, after students have worked together in pairs and small groups and have had a chance to talk out a new skill, they should have opportunities to apply the skill on their own. And in addition to this individual practice, the whole class should work collaboratively on applying the skill, as well as previously-learned skills, in intensive reading lessons. These lessons work best when they are based on issues which interest the class. Articles from the newspaper, a magazine, or a graded reader are useful in many classes. In academically-oriented classes, parts of textbooks and articles from professional journals are excellent choices.

Keeping these guidelines in mind, here is a general lesson plan which works well in conducting interactive classes on reading skills.

Lesson Plan

1. Focus on one reading/thinking skill at a time.

2. Explain the purpose for doing the exercises and how this particular skill is important for effective reading.

3. Do a sample exercise with the whole class. Model aloud your own thinking as you do the exercise.

4. Put the students into pairs (whenever possible and appropriate) and assign one practice exercise.

5. When the pairs have completed the exercise, discuss it with the whole class. Ask how the students arrived at their answers. Encourage friendly disagreement in pairs and in the class as a whole. Ask, "What was your thinking as you decided on that answer?" This means that if there is an answer key, the students are not necessarily "wrong" if they come up with an answer which is different.

6. That day and in the next few classes, assign additional exercises which focus on the same skill, increasing the complexity of the tasks. Make sure the students work together whenever it is feasible.

7. Assign an exercise to be done by individuals, which they will use to check their own ability and confidence in using the skill.

8. Assign further exercises as needed, based on your sense of the students' mastery of the skill.

9. Apply the new skill, and practice previously-mastered skills, in an all-class intensive reading lesson.

→ INTERACTION AND FOCUSING ON THINKING PROCESSES ARE THE KEY FEATURES OF THESE ACTIVITIES. ←

Many teachers have found that the students take a great deal of pride and interest in learning this new approach to reading. In an effort to maintain the focus on skills, it is useful to ask the students to volunteer, from time to time, to name the skills they have been working on, and ask *them* to give *you* an explanation of each skill and a rationale for learning and using the skill in reading English.

The Role of the Teacher in Teaching Reading

Mahon (1986:98–99) states that

> Methodology aside, the teacher is the most important element in a reading class, for her attitude influences students and their performance. The teacher of this component [reading] should provide her students:
>
> 1. an anxiety-free atmosphere so they will feel free to experiment with a new reading style;
> 2. practice so they will master new strategies;
> 3. pressure in the form of persuasion and timings.

But Mahon left out one essential element of the teacher's role, that of *model reader*. Nuttall (1982:192) points out, "Readers are made by readers." She states:

> For disadvantaged students, you may be the only reader they meet — the only person from whom they can 'catch' reading . . . . . *Showing* that you are a reader means carrying books around with you, referring to books as you teach, reading out brief passages that may interest students, talking about what you are reading at the moment, and handling books as if you loved them. *Being* a reader means reading.

Another aspect of this is the teacher's role as model *interpreter*. Since making sense of a text is actually interpretation (Eskey 1986:9), and since so much of the interpretation is cultural (van Dijk and Kintsch 1983; Heath 1984), the teacher's modeling of native-speaker-like comprehending is essential, in class and during individual conferences with students.

Still another aspect of this is the teacher as model *thinker*. Reading is problem solving (see, i.e., Olshavsky 1976), and the teacher can serve as a model by thinking aloud as she introduces new reading skills and strategies.

Organizing Classes and Allocating Time for Various Activities

In order to plan class time effectively, the teacher should take into account which activities are individually assigned and which are worked on by the whole class at once.

Individual Activities

    pleasure reading
    rate building
    developing bottom-up skills and vocabulary
    practicing with materials (such as *Reading for Understanding* — SRA 1965)

Small Group and/or Pair Work
> reading skills exercises
> peer conferences

All-class Activities
> introduction to new skills
> intensive reading lessons
> rate building training (i.e. pacing exercises)

How the reading component of an English course is set up depends on the way classes are organized in particular programs.

a. In an integrated skills class which meets for two to three hours per day, five days per week, allow about 30 minutes per day for reading activities. For instance,

Monday:	Exercises for rate building
Tuesday:	Pleasure reading and book conferences
Wednesday:	Rate building and reading skills
Thursday:	Reading skills exercises
Friday:	Intensive reading lesson or pleasure reading
Homework:	Pleasure reading

b. In an integrated skills class which meets for three hours per week, use about one third of class time for reading activities. In one week, students can complete:

> Four rate building exercises
> Six pages of reading skills exercises
> One intensive reading lesson or pleasure reading
> Homework: Pleasure reading and practice on reading skills exercises

c. In a reading class which meets two hours per week, students can complete these activities in every class:

> Reading skills exercises
> Rate building exercises
> Individual practice
> Pleasure reading and book conferences
> Intensive reading lesson
> Homework: Pleasure reading

Intensive Reading Lessons

Intensive reading lessons are whole-class activities during which the teacher leads the students to apply to a common text those reading skills which they have already learned. The lesson is best designed to include the PreP steps explained on page 41. After each new skill is added to the students' repertoire, an intensive reading lesson should be planned. As the teacher encourages students to select strategies to apply to the text and to monitor their own comprehension, students can develop their metacognitive abilities. This is a very strong combination of process and product.

On the other hand, if a class is required to attempt to apply reading skills which they have not yet learned, an intensive reading lesson can become primarily product-oriented. In such cases, a teacher often "explicates" the text. Students' reading and metacognitive skills do not benefit at all from such a session.

Selecting the right passage for an intensive reading lesson is essential to its success. You should take into account the interests, abilities, and goals of the students. Quite often, newspapers and magazines are good sources of interesting articles. Once students have learned to preview, they can be asked to preview three or four possible texts and then (as a class) select one to use for their intensive reading lesson.

Intensive reading lessons for applying and practicing the skills have been suggested at key points in this book.

B. ACTIVATING BACKGROUND KNOWLEDGE AND CONCEPTUAL FRAMEWORKS

As we noted earlier, bottom-up processing (text-centered, word-by-word reading) is natural when a person first reads a second or foreign language. This is partly due to the reader's own "theory" of how to read, partly the result of a lack of confidence, and partly a realistic response for readers who have acquired very little of a new language.

Students need to learn, therefore, a little about the reading process and especially the fact that it is not the same thing as translating. They also need to learn the importance of their prior knowledge in making sense of a text. In other words, they need to develop their top-down processing mode (Coady 1979).

Many reading skills encourage the use of prior knowledge. In this chapter, we will discuss Previewing and Predicting, two skills which are very important for increasing reading effectiveness, and we will demonstrate a way of systematically applying these skills.

Previewing

Previewing is a high-speed reading skill. It is a powerful skill because by previewing, the reader gains enough information from the text to begin hypothesizing about it and to begin the cognitive process of matching new information with what is already known.

Because most schools introduce new textbooks at the beginning of the semester, it is a good idea to teach previewing as the first reading skill. This will allow the students many opportunities to apply the skill authentically to all of their new texts.

In our daily lives, we preview automatically. When we receive a letter, we check the return address, the postmark, the size and shape of the envelope, the style of the stationery, the handwriting, and other characterictics in a split second before we open it. We want to know what to expect. And when students sign up for a new course, they read the syllabus to find out what to expect during the semester. And before most people decide to read a book, they preview it by reading the front and back covers and maybe the table of contents, and the author's name; they note the book's length and other features. But many students, who may preview some things in their personal lives, neglect this important previewing step when they read school materials.

Note: Before working on a skill for the first time, always begin with a *rationale* for doing the exercises. Explain what the skill is and why it can improve reading ability in English. This helps the students put the skill in context and builds conscious awareness of the skill as a strategy to use whenever it is required. Throughout this book, Sample Rationales are given for each skill. These are suggested explanations beginning with the one below.

Sample Rationale

Before you go on a trip, you probably look at a map in order to have some idea about the trip. You want to know what kind of roads you will drive on, which cities or towns you will pass through, how long it will take, and whether or not there are any interesting sights along the way. This helps you enjoy the trip.

Before you read, it is a good idea to find out about what you will read. If you look over (preview) the text before you read, you will help yourself understand and remember what you read.

Steps in Previewing

1. Read the title.
2. Look at any pictures.
3. Notice if the text is divided into parts.
4. Read the first sentence of each paragraph.
5. Read the last paragraph or at least the last sentence.
6. Notice names, numbers, dates, and words that stand out.

Introducing the Skill of Previewing

Here is a good way to introduce the skill of previewing and to emphasize how much the students already know before they read:

Assign a chapter from one of the *Timed Readings* books (Spargo and Williston 1980) or from any collection of short selections which are followed by about ten questions. Tell the students that they will have two minutes to preview. Then tell them to answer the questions *without reading the passage.*

This activity usually amazes the students, because they often find they can answer several of the questions correctly without even reading the passage! Many students gain confidence from this demonstration.

On the other hand, some students do not agree that guessing is "really reading," and they say that they think guessing is "cheating." It is important to discuss this issue with the class, because, in fact, accessing background knowledge and guessing make it possible to be an effective reader. You can point out that the students understand and remember what they read because of their prior knowledge and because of their ability to guess.

Sample Exercise B.1. Previewing

Note: From the daily paper, select a news story which reports on an event. Try to find a story accompanied by a photograph.

Directions: Preview this news story. You will have 1 minute. Then work with a partner and answer these questions:

a. What is the article about?

b. What kind of text is it?

c. What do you already know about this?

d. Is the story difficult for you?

e. What are some of the names, dates, numbers, or other important words you noticed.

f. Did you learn anything new? What?

Discussion: Ask each pair to report to the class about their preview of the story.

Previewing a Textbook

Previewing is especially relevant if students are using textbooks in their other classes. Students can learn to improve their study skills by applying the previewing skill to a textbook which they are currently using, or you can provide a collection of sample textbooks from several different fields of study. It is a good idea to begin by demonstrating how to preview a textbook for the whole class, so that students will understand how much useful information they can obtain from a brief preview.

How to Preview a Textbook

1. Read the title page and the copyright page. Find the author's name(s) and the date of publication. This information is important because it allows the reader to make a judgement about how up-to-date the book might be.

2. Read the table of contents. Check the organization of the book, the number of sections, the number of chapters.

3. Scan the first chapter. Look for illustrations, charts, tables; read the headings; check to see if there is an end-of-chapter summary or discussion questions. The students should understand that it is not "cheating" to read the end of the chapter first.

4. Look at the first page of each chapter and/or part of the book.

5. Skim quickly through the final chapter. The students should be aware that the final chapter is often a conclusion which ties a book together.

6. Examine the materials at the back of the book. Check to see if there is an index, a glossary (especially important for second language learners), bibliography, charts and tables, or other aids.

Sample Exercise B.2. Previewing Your Own Textbook

Directions: Preview your textbook. Answer these questions. Tell another student about your textbook.

1. Title

2. Author (s)

3. Date of publication

4. Number of pages

5. Check the features. Does your textbook contain

   ____ a table of contents?

   ____ an index?

   ____ a glossary?

   ____ a bibliography?

   ____ end-of-chapter questions?

   ____ illustrations?

   ____ charts and graphs?

   ____ anything else helpful to the reader?

Discussion: Each student will report on a textbook, and evaluate it on its features. Students can discover how textbooks from different fields are different in the way the text is presented.

Previewing Chapters of Books

Students should also learn how to preview parts of a book. Ask the students to bring in a textbook from another class for this exercise. In previewing a chapter, the students should be instructed to follow these steps:

How to Preview a Textbook Chapter

1. Read the title.
2. Look at all of the illustrations.
3. If the chapter is divided into parts, scan the headings.
4. Very quickly read the first and last paragraphs of the chapter.
5. Very quickly read the summary or discussion questions at the end of the chapter, if there are any.

Previewing Articles and Essays

To demonstrate this, you may wish to choose an essay which can serve as the basis for a class discussion, i.e., an opinion essay from *Time* Magazine. Once again, the students should have only one or two minutes to preview. Be sure to remind them of the steps in previewing as listed above.

Previewing Books for Pleasure Reading

It is a good idea for the class to take trips to the library and to bookstores to browse and to find new books to read. But this may be a new experience for many students, and they may need instruction in how to preview books for personal reading.

You can introduce this kind of previewing in class. Bring in a big bag of paperback books and do the following exercise. (Remember to give the students *a very strict time limit* when they preview.)

Sample Exercise B.3.

Directions: Choose a book. You will have five minutes to preview the book. Use the checklist below to find out all you can about the book. Then tell another student about the book.

Checklist of key features:

____ Title _____

____ Author _____

____ Type of book

        fiction _____ non-fiction _____

____ What's it about? _____

_____

____ Date of publication _____

____ Length of book _____ pages

____ Print easy to read _____ yes _____ no _____

____ Front and back cover materials

Discussion: Did all books have all of these features?
                Would you like to read this book? Why?

(During the class discussion of the books and their features, it is a good idea to make sure that students understand the meaning and the significance of all of the features. They may not realize, for example, that very small print will make their eyes tired and discourage them from reading.)

Benefits of Previewing

1. Previewing allows the reader to establish the genre, context, topic, level of difficulty, and organization of the text to be read.

2. Once aware of the topic, the students' activated background knowledge allows them to read for meaning, even if many of the words in the text are unfamiliar.

3. Students realize once again that it is not necessary to read every word in order to understand and gain information from a text.

4. Previewing trains the students in the habit of a quick "once-over" before reading, the groundwork for learning to skim, a much more complicated task.

Once the students have learned to preview, the previewing step should be included whenever the students are given a reading assignment. Each time the class begins a new book (i.e., grammar, vocabulary), they should take a few minutes to preview the text before they begin to use it.

Predicting

Because teachers often ask students to predict before they read in class, they may assume that students will also predict when they read on their own. That's not necessarily so!

Predicting should be introduced as a specific skill. As always, the introduction of a new skill requires a rationale.

Sample Rationale

Before you read, you can do something to improve your understanding. You can guess what will be in the passage. This is called *predicting*. When there is a title, a picture, or some other information about what you will read, stop and think!

When you *predict*, you find out:

a. what kind of text you will read. Is it a newspaper article, a story, an advertisement, a textbook, a recipe, a letter, or what?

b. what you already know about what you will read.

c. how carefully you want to read it. Will you read to remember every word? Will you scan, for one or two pieces of information? Will you read for pleasure, with no need to remember?

In practice, we know that predicting is usually unconscious and is done prior to reading. But for the purpose of highlighting the *process* of predicting, it is necessary to give the students some training with exercises which isolate the skill. Naturally, students should be instructed to apply the skill whenever they read, and predicting should be an explicit part of all-class, intensive reading lessons.

Sample Exercise B.4. Predicting from Pictures

Note: For this exercise, find large illustrations from several interesting magazine articles, i.e. *National Geographic* or *Time*.

Directions: Work in small groups (four or five students). Look at this picture from a magazine article.

What will be in this article?

What kind of article is this?

What do you already know about this?

Discussion: Did all the groups agree?

Sample Exercise B.5. Making a Story from Pictures

Note: Although this type of exercise is often used as a speaking/writing activity, it is also very useful for making students aware of the importance of using illustrations to predict what they might read in a text. The pictures should be interesting and relevant to the class. Sources include comic strips and news magazines.

Directions: Look at this set of pictures. They can be used to make a story. Work in a small group of three to five students. Put the pictures in order to make a story.

Discussion: Compare what each group produces. Ask them to explain to each other any differences or similarities.

Sample Exercise B.6. Predicting from a Table of Contents

Contents

from *NISA: The Life and Words of a !Kung Woman* by Marjorie Shostak

What is this?
What can you predict about the book?

Directions: Work in a small group. Make at least five predictions about the book.

Discussion: Each group reports their predictions and explains their reasons for making them.

Sample Exercise B.7. Predicting from Titles and Headlines

Directions: Here are five newspaper stories and five headlines. Read each head-line. Predict the story. Find the matching story. Work in a small group of three to five students.

(*Note:* If the size of the print might give away the match, it's a good idea to type out the headlines instead of handing out the originals.)

Discussion: Students should compare their matchings, and talk about how they made their decisions.

Sample Exercise B.8. Predicting from a Title (For beginning level students)

Directions: Will you find these ideas in the story? Check yes or no. Work with another student. Be ready to give a reason for your answer.

Boston: A Good Place to Live

	Yes	No
1. There are many poor people in Boston.	____	____
2. The spring flowers are beautiful in Boston.	____	____
3. There are many universities in Boston.	____	____
4. Jobs are hard to find in the Boston area.	____	____
5. Winters in Boston are cold and snowy.	____	____
6. Boston City Hall is very beautiful.	____	____
7. There are many famous old buildings in downtown Boston.	____	____
8. People are not very friendly in Boston.	____	____
9. The Charles River flows by the city. People like to walk along the river in the parks.	____	____
10. Apartments are very expensive and hard to find.	____	____

(from *Reading Power*)

Sample Exercise B.9. Predicting What Will Come Next in a Story.

Note: This idea is taken from Grellet's book, *Developing Reading Skills* (1981). Select a short story with a fairly clear sequence of events. (Grellet used "The Unicorn in the Garden," by James Thurber.) Cut the story into separate strips, so that the students can physically re-assemble it. Read the first strip aloud. With the students in small groups, give each student one strip. Each group should have a complete set of strips. Their task is to put the story together in its original order.

This is a good predicting exercise, because as students propose which part of the story they think should come next, they have to explain their reasons to the other students in their group. Articulating their reasons reinforces their awareness of the role of predicting in reading. This exercise also gives the students an opportunity to read aloud in an authentic fashion, as each group reads and re-reads its strips in order to put them in the correct sequence. The stories can be simple folk tales, fairy tales, or children's stories which might not otherwise find their way into the classroom. For beginning-level ESL/EFL students, the teacher should be sure that the story is a very simple one. This exercise is more difficult than it appears to be.

Directions: These strips are parts of a story. Each person in your group should have one strip. Read your own strip silently. The teacher will read the first part of the story to you. (strip d.) Then each student will read a strip out loud to the others, and the group will decide the correct order of the strips. Write the best order for the strips:

1. _____   2. _____   3. _____   4. _____   5. _____   6. _____   7. _____

Story in strips:

The Stolen Car

---

d. A car thief at Boston's Logan Airport got more than he expected last week. The car he decided to steal was not empty.

---

f. A two year old girl and two poodle dogs were asleep in the back seat.

---

b. Greg Winter, the father of the child, left the car for just a minute. He ran into the terminal building to bring a lunch to his wife, Susan.

---

a. When he came out of the terminal, he was dismayed . . . . . his car was gone!

---

c. Greg called the police and went with them in a search of the area around the airport.

---

e. The car (with child and dogs still safe inside) was found in less than two hours.

---

g. The thief, apparently recognizing his mistake, had abandoned the car in East Boston.

PreP: Making Semantic Associations

PreP (Pre-reading Preparatory Instruction — Langer, 1981) is another way to help students activate concepts and background knowledge before they read, and it provides a systematic way to apply the skills of previewing and predicting. PreP is a "pre-reading plan intended to make readers aware of what they already know about a topic to be read about and to activate their memory and expectations," (Schulz 1983). It is a form of brainstorming. Students can learn to follow the PreP steps before they read alone, and PreP can be included in the pre-reading activity before an all-class intensive reading lesson.

PreP consists of three phases. The procedure requires almost no teacher preparation, and it can be used with any text at every language proficiency level. PreP also provides the teacher with reliable feedback for estimating the students' conceptual and linguistic background knowledge about a topic.

The PreP Procedure

1. Select a key word, phrase, or picture from the text which will stimulate group discussion. (This is not the same as pre-teaching important words from a text. The key word does not even have to appear in the text.) Ask the students to make associations with this word, phrase or picture. List all of their associations on the chalkboard.

2. The students tell the reasons for the associations they have made. This reflecting step activates a network of additional associations; as they discuss their initial associations, students will be reminded of other related ideas (Schulz 1983).

3. Ask the students for additional associations which have come to mind during the discussion and write these on the chalkboard as well.

Langer (1981), who introduced this procedure, found that "the three levels of response elicited by the PreP not only help the students to comprehend a text, but greatly facilitate the student's ability to recall the text after reading."

Students should understand why the PreP procedure is useful and what they gain from doing it. In order to stress this, ask your students to evaluate the procedure after they have done it several times. Point out the ways PreP helps students to think and predict before they read, and how such thinking assists in comprehending and remembering.

Students can also do PreP in pairs, using a PreP worksheet that you have devised. Using the title, an accompanying illustration, or the first sentence of the passage as the catalyst, two or three students can perform the steps of associating, reflecting, and further associating together.

Sample Rationale

Sometimes you know a lot more about what you are reading than you think you do! You know about the ideas in your own language. It is the new language which, at first, may make you think you are reading about something totally new to you.

PreP is a way of remembering what you already know. Before you read, you should stop and think about the ideas in the passage. Then you will understand and remember more of what you read.

Sample Exercise B.10. Making Associations

Note: Many students may have little or no experience with free association. An exercise like this can introduce this activity. Use stimulus words which are appropriate for your students.

Directions: Tell the class what you think of when you see this word.

School

(Write each association on the board.)

Directions:
On the worksheet, you will find ten words. On the line next to each word, write the first thing you think of. Then compare your associations with a partner.

Making Associations

1. doctor _____

2. ice cream _____

3. television _____

4. war _____

5. book _____

6. New York _____

7. zoo _____

8. hungry _____

9. music _____

10. job _____

Class should then discuss their lists. Were they similar? Why? Why not?

Sample Exercise B.11.

Directions: Work with two other students. Follow the steps of PreP. Each student should make as many associations as you can about this:

Being Afraid in the Dark

1. Write a list of all of your associations. Write every idea that you think of.
2. Read your lists to each other. Explain why you thought of your associations. Are all of the lists alike?
3. Now think again, and write any new associations you have thought of.
4. Did you find you had more ideas about these words?

Applying Previewing, Predicting, and PreP

The following lesson applies these three skills in a model intensive reading lesson (Bonesteel 1986).

1. Distribute a one- or two-page passage to the class. It should be a selection which is not too difficult, although it does not have to be easy. In this exercise, even beginning classes can get something out of a passage which might ordinarily be too difficult. It is important that the passage be interesting and attractive.
2. Tell the students to preview the passage for about two or three minutes.
3. Then tell the students to put the passages aside and ask them to tell what they remember from the preview. Write all of their ideas on the chalkboard and discuss, following the PreP procedure outlined above.
4. Next, tell the students to predict what else they might find when they read the passage, based on what they have collectively seen in the preview. Students give reasons for their predictions. These are, in effect, the further associations of PreP.
5. Then assign about ten true/false questions about the text.
6. After they have answered the true/false questions, instruct the students to read the entire article, looking for confirmation of their predictions and for verification of their answers to the questions.
7. Finally, give the whole class a chance to discuss the extent to which their predictions proved to be accurate, and why or why not.

Many different kinds of passages can be used in this lesson. Often there are interesting selections in readers which already have true-false questions accompanying them. Other good sources are *Parade Magazine, People*, the newspaper, some of the popular special-interest magazines, and news magazines. (Of course, you will have to write the true/false questions for these.)

Benefits of This Lesson Plan

This lesson plan is one which could be included in every intensive reading lesson, because student interaction and student/teacher interaction are essential in such lessons. When you explain your own thinking processes, students have an opportunity to discover new ways of thinking about a text. As the students work together, predicting and making associations about a text, they practice the thinking processes involved in relating the text to what they already know. Once they have practiced talking this way together, it is possible for them to internalize these processes and apply them when they read alone.

Intensive Reading Lesson

At this point, plan an intensive reading lesson. Using a text selected for its interest to the class, guide the students in their application of the Previewing and Predicting skills. It is a good idea to do the PreP steps in every intensive reading lesson.

C. LEARNING NOT TO READ EVERY WORD

Many students read very slowly, one word at a time. Second language students read word by word, translating silently to their first language as they proceed. This practice may lead to a feeling of security, because students may believe that if they know every word, they know the meaning of the text. Of course, that is not necessarily the case. As we have seen, the reader derives meaning by applying prior knowledge to the printed text. Students will not necessarily understand a text just because they have translated every single word.

It is often difficult for a teacher to convince students to stop reading word by word and to guess or even skip words they do not know. In this chapter, several direct approaches are suggested for addressing this issue in the classroom:

1. Cloze exercises can demonstrate to students that they can read and understand a text without attending to every word.

2. The skill of scanning, a high-speed reading skill, can show that it is sometimes *necessary* to skip many words in reading for specific information.

3. Training in reading faster can make it physically impossible for students to read every word. Pressure to speed up forces the reader to chunk (take in groups of words) and to skim over parts of the text.

Eventually, students will be able to risk skipping over unknown words and unimportant parts of texts as they develop confidence in their ability to apply the reading skills and strategies shown in this book. With all of these approaches, the cardinal rule is that students will learn best if they *experience* the activity, not just *hear* about it.

Exercises Based on the Principle of Closure

Cloze Passages

Cloze passages are familiar to many teachers. In a cloze passage, the first sentence is left intact, and then words are systematically deleted (i.e., every 5th word, every 7th word). Cloze exercises can be used to determine text readability (the original use by Taylor, in 1953), and to teach many aspects of language, including grammar and vocabulary. (For further discussion of the cloze procedure, see the Appendix.)

Cloze passages can also be used to demonstrate the fact that in English it is possible to understand a passage without reading every word. Even with 18% or more of the words missing, students will discover that they can understand and even answer comprehension questions about a passage. (If the topic is a very familiar one, probably 90% of a text could be eliminated, and still the students could "read" it.)

It should be kept in mind, as Eskey (1973) pointed out, that when students are required to write words in the blank spaces, the cloze exercise is a vocabulary or grammar task. Therefore, in using cloze as we do here, the students need to be reminded that what matters is *not* providing the missing words, but understanding the text *in spite of* the missing words.

Using Cloze Reading Exercises to Encourage Guessing

You can use these exercises to demonstrate to your students that they do not have to read every word in order to comprehend a passage. As always, begin with a *rationale* for doing the exercises.

Sample Rationale

In order to raise the issue of word-by-word reading, ask your students to respond to this questionnaire:

Reading Questionnaire

True or False?

1. It is important to read every word if you want to understand.
2. You will learn more if you stop and look up every new word in the dictionary.
3. You should be able to say every word as you read.
4. If you read fast, you will not understand.
5. You should write the words in your own language above the English words when you read.

(Adapted from Mahon 1986)

These are all *FALSE*, but students often argue that many are true. A class discussion of this questionnaire will provide you with an opportunity to explain the reasons for not reading every word.

These cloze reading exercises will help you convince your students that they do not have to read every word in order to comprehend a text. Be sure to select passages which are simple for the students to understand. They should have no trouble answering a few comprehension questions about the passages. Start with a passage from which you have deleted every 10th word. Then assign passages from which you have deleted every 7th word and every 5th word.

Sample Exercise C.1. (Every 10th word deleted)

Directions: Read the passage. *Do not write the missing words.* Answer the questions.

Dennis and Linda Wilson are married. They have three children. Dennis works full-time, but Linda _____ not work away from home. The Wilson family needs _____ money for clothes and food. Dennis wants to get _____ part-time job on Saturday. Linda wants to work, too. _____ does not want Linda to work. He wants her _____ stay home to clean the house and to take _____ care of the children.

1. Do Dennis and Linda both work? _____

2. Does the family have a problem about money? _____

3. Who cleans the house? _____

4. Who earns the money? _____

(Adapted from *Impact! Book 1*)

Note: Mahon (1986) suggests that after the students answer the questions, the class should discuss the missing words. They can tell which word belongs in each blank and why they think so.

Sample Exercise C.2. (Every 7th word deleted)

Directions: Read the passage. Answer the questions. Do not write the missing words.

Catalog Shopping

Many people like catalog shopping. They shop at home and use _____ gas in their cars. They also _____ less time to shop and have _____ time to relax. And they say _____ are cheaper in catalogs than in _____.

1. Everybody likes catalog shopping.	Yes No
2. Everybody likes shopping in stores.	Yes No
3. People have different ideas about shopping.	Yes No

(Adapted from *Impact! Book 2*)

Sample Exercise C.3. (Every 5th word deleted)

Directions: Read the passage. Do not write the missing words. Answer the questions.

Barbara Willis doesn't need to own a car. She is 40 years _____, single, and a school _____. She doesn't earn much _____, but she likes to _____ a lot. She often _____ a car. She prefers _____ rent a car on _____ because the prices are _____. She also usually rents _____ car for several weeks _____ the summer because she _____ to take a vacation _____.

1. Barbara Willis is married.	Yes	No
2. Barbara likes to travel.	Yes	No
3. Barbara often rents a car.	Yes	No

(Adapted from *Impact! Book 2*)

Longer passages with comprehension questions already written (for example, passages from readers) can also be used for cloze reading exercises. In the sample below (a passage from *Reading Power*, a beginning level reading skills text), every 5th word has been deleted. The comprehension questions were written before the deletions were made.

Sample Exercise C.4.

Directions: Read the passage but *do not fill in the missing words.* Answer the questions.

All around the world, people drink tea. But tea does not _____ the same thing to _____. In different countries people _____ very different ideas about _____ tea.

In China, for _____, tea is always served _____ people get together. The _____ drink it any time _____ day, at home or _____ teahouses. They prefer their _____ plain, with nothing else _____ it.

Tea is also _____ in Japan. The Japanese _____ a special way of _____ tea called a tea _____. It is very old _____ full of meaning. Everything _____ be done in a _____ way in the ceremony. _____ is even a special _____ for it in Japanese _____.

Another tea-drinking country is _____. In England, the late _____ is "teatime." Almost everyone _____ a cup of tea then. _____ English usually make tea _____ a teapot and drink _____ with cream and sugar. _____ also eat cakes, cookies, _____ little sandwiches at teatime.

_____ the United States people _____ tea mostly for breakfast _____ after meals. Americans usually _____ tea bags to make _____ tea. Tea bags are _____ and easier than making _____ in teapots. In the _____, many Americans drink cold _____ — "iced tea." They sometimes _____ iced tea from cans, _____ soda.

Circle the best answer:

1. This passage is about
   a. Chinese tea
   b. how tea is important
   c. English teatime
   d. different ways of drinking tea in different countries

2. Tea is popular
   a. all around the world
   b. only in the United States
   c. only in English-speaking countries
   d. in Asian countries

3. The Chinese drink tea
   a. for breakfast
   b. in a special ceremony
   c. when they get together
   d. only in teahouses

4. The tea ceremony is a
   a. kind of Japanese tea
   b. special way of serving tea in Japan
   c. kind of restaurant
   d. special time of the afternoon

5. Teatime in England is
   a. in the evening
   b. in the morning
   c. after dinner
   d. in the afternoon

6. The English like to
   a. eat cakes and cookies with their tea
   b. drink their tea plain
   c. have tea with dinner
   d. drink their tea in a special room

7. Americans usually
   a. make tea in teapots
   b. drink tea in restaurants
   c. make tea from tea bags
   d. do not drink tea

8. Iced tea is popular
   a. in the winter
   b. in England
   c. for breakfast
   d. in the United States

(*Adapted from Reading Power*)

Many other kinds of materials can be used for cloze reading exercises. Grellet (1981) recommends using examples from everyday life: postcards which have gotten smudged in the mail, with half the words illegible; titles on very old copies of books, with many of the letters in the titles missing. Horoscopes, instructions for completing a process, descriptions of places, or narratives are also useful. The teacher's goal is to convince students that they can infer the meaning of a text even if they do not read every word.

Scanning

Scanning is a high-speed reading skill used for locating specific information. Scanning is often confused with skimming, a much more complicated skill demanding a greater degree of language knowledge and reading skill to perform effectively. Skimming is discussed in a later section.

Scanning is a very important and useful skill for all readers. When students learn to scan, they learn that they can obtain information from a text without reading every word. In addition, they develop the ability to visualize words in English as they scan for them. And they learn that they can use scanning as a strategy for speeding up their sampling of any text.

It is important that students understand that scanning is an *extremely* high speed reading activity and that they should *not* try to read the entire passage carefully. In order to make sure that the students are actually scanning and not reading every word, introduce scanning exercises by reading aloud the request for information which is to be found by scanning, rather than having each student read questions silently and then scan for the answers.

Many teachers have found that if they make scanning exercises into competitions, either between two groups of students or between everyone in the class, the students are more willing to risk skipping over many words in the text to find the information required. The success of this use of competition will depend, of course, on the background of the students and their familiarity with (and acceptance of) competitive activities.

Teacher-Designed Materials

As with cloze exercises, many different texts can be used for scanning practice, but current, interesting material is best, i.e., newspaper ads, magazine articles, catalogs. The most exciting and productive scanning exercises are those which the teacher designs, because they can be geared to the ages and interests of the students in the class. Successful scanning lessons have been based on restaurant menus, TV program schedules, articles from *Time* and *Newsweek*, restaurant reviews, movie listings, and most popular of all, classified ads.

In a scanning lesson, you can ask many different kinds of questions. The best questions are those which you write with a specific class in mind. (For instance, the scanning exercise can serve simultaneously as a review of wh-questions.) By varying the questions, the same material can be used for students with widely differing proficiencies in English. (For example, two levels of questions are presented in Sample Exercise C.5.)

Sample Rationale

When you need information from a newspaper or a book, you do not need to read every word.

Today we will work on a reading skill called scanning. This is a very high speed skill.

You can scan whenever you need a piece of information from a text. For example, if you need to find someone's telephone number, you do not read the whole telephone directory! You read only what you need. Can you think of any other times you can scan? (Students will probably mention schedules, indexes, ads, and dictionaries.) You can improve your reading in English if you learn to scan and read only the words you need.

Sample Exercise C.5. Capsule Movie Reviews

Note: This is an all-class activity. Explain the directions for doing the exercise before handing out copies of the movie listings, because students should not have an opportunity to read them before the scanning exercise begins. Read the questions aloud to the class and emphasize speed. Most classes enjoy scanning exercises which are conducted as contests between halves of the group. A team scores a point when they are first with the *accurate answer.*

Directions: This is a list of short reviews of movies. Reviews give information about the movies, where to see them, and their rating. Do not look at the reviews until I tell you to do so. When I ask a question, *scan* the page and locate the answer as quickly as you can. Raise your hand when you have the answer.
Speed is important!

MOVIES

CAPSULE REVIEWS

Movies are rated from one to four stars by Globe film critics.
★★★★ Excellent; ★★★ Good
★★ Passable; ★ Poor

Films will be shown at locations given at the end of each capsule review. See Movie Houses for film days and times.
★ **"The Allnighter"** — Susanna Hoffs of the Bangles makes her film debut in a lethargic, lame and leaden yarn about students at the end of their college years. (PG-13) *See Brockton, Burlington, Revere*

★★★★ **"Betty Blue"** — Jean-Jacques Beineix recovers the form that launched him in "Diva," masters the artiness that mastered him in "Moon in the Gutter," and stylishly hitches it to an arresting story of obsessive love. Newcomer Beatrice Dalle is a standout as the mad muse of a rejected writer. *See Copley Place, Boston; Newton*

★ **"Beverly Hills Cop II"** — II too many. (R) *See Cinema 57, Boston; Danvers, Dedham, Falmouth, Framingham, Newton, Pembroke, Revere, Somerville, Weymouth, Woburn.*

★★★★ **"Black Widow"** — Director Bob Rafelson's stunning, steamy, sexy thriller is marked by great performance by Theresa Russell as the murderous widow and Debra Winger as a Justice Department investigater. The best thriller in years. (R) *See Needham.*

★★★★ **"Blue Velvet"** — It begins when young clean-cut Kyle MacLachlan finds a severed human ear in a weed-covered lot. He kisses white-picket-fence America good-bye as he finds, to his horror, that something in him wants to play nightmare games with the seething dope pusher behind all the evil. This is the film we knew director David Lynch had in him ever since he surfaced with "Eraserhead." It's bizarre, exhilarating, stylish and original — literally and figuratively the American underworld film of the decade. (R) *See Newburyport, Somerville.*

★★★ **"The Color of Money"** — Director Martin Scorsese, screenwriter Richard Price, cinematographer Michael Ballhaus and stars Paul Newman and Tom Cruise, in a follow-up to "The Hustler," have created the best sequel since "The Godfather II." (R) *See Beacon Hill, Boston*

★★★★ **"Cutter's Way"** — Ivan Passer's brilliant evocation of the American Dream turned nightmare is a first-rate thriller with superb performances by John Heard and Jeff Bridges. But it's more than that. Like a cinematic Herman Melville, Passer integrates historical, literary and psychological symbols into his riveting narrative. One of the best films of any year. (R) *See Somerville.*

★★ **"Evil Dead II"** — Not for the faint of heart, but definitely for those interested in seeing how director Sam Raimi transforms a mediocre script into a successful spoof of splatter movies. (R) *See Pi Alley, Boston*

★ **"Extreme Prejudice"** — Walter Hill tries for an '80s Western. Whether Texas Ranger Nick Nolte will team up with his old buddy, now a dope king, or with six kill-crazy soldiers hunting the dope king, becomes unimportant as the film veers off into bullet-riddled Sergio Leone territory. (R) *See Beacon Hill, Boston*

★★★★ **"The Fly"** — Jeff Goldblum stars in this gory, horrifying metamorphosis of man to insect. As they said in the ad for the original — not for the squeamish. (R) *See Brookline.*

★★ **"Gardens of Stone"** — An honorable, if flawed, attempt to show the effect of the Vietnam War on the men back home, in this case, grizzled vets James Caan and James Earl Jones, both assigned to bury their dead in Arlington National Cemetery. (R) *See Paris, Boston; Harvard Square, Cambridge; Braintree, Brockton, Burlington, Danvers, Hanover, Lawrence, Milford, Natick, Revere, and Somerville*

★ **"The Gate"** — A laughable, so-called horror flick about a suburban couple with a teen-age daughter, a grade school son and a hole in the backyard that serves as "gate to the domain of demons who once ruled the Earth." (PG-14) *See Allston, Cinema 57, Boston; Brockton, Burlington, Danvers, Dedham, Framingham, Lawrence, Revere, Somerville*

★ **"Gothic"** — Ken Russell's long, hectic, campy, empty music video about Byron, Shelley and their set knocking back laudahum, behaving like sex fiends, and creating Frankenstein on a dark, stormy night in Switzerland in 1816. (R) *See Pi Alley, Boston*

★★★ **"Hoosiers"** — "Rocky" in quintuplicate, as a 1951 smalltown high school basketball team battles the odds in Indiana. The authentic Hoosier setting counts for a lot here. So do Gene Hackman, Dennis Hopper and Barbara Hershey in the Gipper film of the decade. (PG) *See Village Cinema, Boston; Arlington, Randolph.*

★★ **"Ishtar"** — One star for Dustin Hoffman and one for Warren Beatty. None for writer-director Elaine May. (PG-13) *See Cheri, Boston; Braintree, Brockton, Brookline, Danvers, Lawrance, Milford, Norwell, Revere, Somerville, Woburn.*

★★ **"Kangaroo"** — Ungainly film version of D. H. Lawrence's novel about Australia. Worth seeing, though, for Judy Davis's wonderfully tangy portrayal of Lawrence's wife, Frieda. (R) *See Copley Place, Boston*

★★ **"Man Facing Southeast"** — This leaden import is filled with weighty messages at the expense of drama. The film's about as compelling as the title makes it sound. *See Copley, Boston*

★ "Meduses" — So bad that it even makes looking at naked women boring. (R) *See Copley Place, Boston; Harvard Square, Cambridge; Brookline, Lexington, Natick.*

★★★ "Men ..." — A cool, bemused comedy from Germany about male bonding, and, beyond that, about the ways we don't like to admit that the romantic and the conforming souls often fuse. That's what happens when a Munich ad man sets out to sabotage his wife's bohemian lover. Light, lively, warmed by generosity. *See Brookline.*

★★★★ "My Sweet Little Village" — Jiri Menzel's winning Czech comedy of village intrigues that owes a lot to classic American silent film, especially in its central characters, a whooping crane version of Stan Laurel named Otik and a compressed, short-fused Hardy named Pavek. *See Newton*

★★ "Project X" — Matthew Broderick, as an Air Force lab assistant, talks to the animals, especially a chimp named Virgil. This pro-animal-rights film, which centers around Broderick's efforts to keep the chimp from being zapped by a dangerous experiment, is appealingly gentle, but ultimately too tame. (PG) *See Beacom Hill, Boston; Braintree, Brockton, Brookline, Hanover, Lawrence, Natick, Peabody, Revere, Somerville*

★★★ "Raising Arizona" — The brother team of Joel and Ethan Coen push pop art into slapstick surrealism as a childless couple kidnaps a baby, with hectic consequences. The camerawork calls too much attention to its film-school cleverness, but the film's warm, loopy energies and its sympathetic performances by Nicolas Cage and Holly Hunter carry it. (PG-13) *See Cheri, Boston, Harvard Square, Cambridge; Brockton, Dedham, Framingham, Hanover, Newton, Woburn*

Movie Industry Ratings:
    G = General Audience
  PG = Parental Guidance suggested; some material may not be suitable to pre-teenagers
PG-13 = Parents cautioned to give special guidance for attendance of children under 13
    R = Restricted; under age 17 requires accompanying parent or adult guardian
    X = No one under 17 admitted

Scanning questions: Beginning and Low Intermediate Level

1. What does three stars mean?
2. Who can attend an X-rated movie?
3. What is the Movie Industry Rating for *The Gate*?
4. Are there any X-rated movies listed?
5. Is *Kangaroo* a good film for children?
6. Is *Project X* an excellent film?
7. Where can I see *Cutter's Way*?
8. Where is *Raising Arizona* being shown?
9. How many theaters are showing *Blue Velvet*?
10. How many of the films listed are considered excellent?

(*Note:* It is a good idea to include simple questions like those above even in advanced classes, because there is usually a wide range of scanning ability in every class.)

Scanning questions: High Intermediate and Advanced Level

1. Which film is set in Australia?
2. In which film does a man become an insect?
3. Who are the actors in *Hoosiers*?
4. Who are the stars in *Black Widow*?
5. Which film is about a small Czech town?
6. Which film is directed by David Lynch?
7. Which film features chimpanzees?
8. Who is the director of *Ishtar*?
9. Which film stars Paul Newman?
10. What is the title of the German comedy?

Using Published Materials for Scanning Practice

Published materials are also available for teaching scanning. For example, *Skimming and Scanning* (Fry 1981), is a workbook which includes a nice introduction to the scanning process and many exercises using materials from daily life. However, when students work on such exercises alone, they almost always slow down and read the entire passage carefully, thus defeating the purpose. Fry's book is best used for whole-class activities, with the teacher reading the questions aloud. Alternatively, the students can be paired, and can take turns reading the questions aloud and timing each other. Another option is to allow the students to work independently, but under *strictly timed conditions*.

Reading Power (Mikulecky and Jeffries 1986) includes a section on scanning for beginning level students. Here is an exercise based on a newspaper advertisement.

Sample Exercise C.6.
SCANNING A NEWSPAPER AD
Scan the ad below to find the answers to these questions. Work very fast.

Starting time _____

1. Which computer has the lowest price? _____
2. What do you get free with the Process Partner? _____
3. What is the name of the computer store? _____
4. How many computer courses can you take at DSI? _____
5. Does the PaqComp run BIM programs? _____
6. What is the price of the Partner 384K memory? _____

Finishing time _____
Scanning time _____

Some reading labs and classrooms are supplied with a set of *Rate Builders*, reading cards published by Science Research Associates (SRA) and usually used for reading rate improvement practice. These materials are also useful for teaching and practicing scanning.

Each *Rate Builder* card consists of a short passage followed by several questions. Because many of the questions are literal, students can readily locate the answers *without* reading the passage. Students should be instructed to answer the questions on the *Rate Builder* card by scanning the passage very rapidly. Since each card is different, students will have to work independently, but if the teacher imposes a very short time limit (two minutes maximum), the students will not have time to read every word in the passage.

Sample Exercise C.7.
Rate Builder

A hermit crab that has found an empty shell for its new home may share its dwelling. It chooses a sea anemone to settle on top of the shell. This flowerlike animal's usual home is on a rock.

The sea anemone gains by the partnership. As it rides on the shell, it has a better chance of getting food. Pieces of food torn by the crab as it dines may also reach the anemone's mouth.

The crab profits in its turn. Its enemies find the crab harder to see and to attack. Around the anemone's mouth are tiny arms called tentacles. These shoot out threads that poison and even kill.

A hermit crab sometimes becomes a "two-gun" wandered. It carries an anemone on each claw of its first pair of legs.

1. The crab in this partnership is the
   a. spider crab
   b. fiddler crab
   c. hermit crab
   d. sponge crab

2. Its partner is described as
   a. a sea plant
   b. a sea flower
   c. an animallike flower
   d. a flowerlike animal

3. The crab's partner lives
   a. inside the shell
   b. on top of the shell
   c. on a nearby rock
   d. None of the above

4. The sea anemone gains because it has a better
   a. supply of food
   b. place to hide
   c. Both A and B
   d. Neither A nor B

5. The crab gains because it is
   a. better hidden from its enemies
   b. protected by the anemone's tentacles
   c. Both A and B
   d. Neither A nor B

6. A "two-gun" crab is protected by
   a. two anemones settled on its shell
   b. an anemone on each foreclaw
   c. an anemone on each of its hindmost pair of legs
   d. two guns

7. In the crab-anaemone relationship, the two animals
   a. both profit while living together
   b. work together only now and then
   c. try to harm each other
   d. each use tentacles against enemies

Reading Faster

Some teachers may be surprised when they hear that they should teach their students to read faster. However, there are both pedagogical and practical reasons for including reading rate improvement in the reading class, even for ESL/EFL students.

First, working on increasing their reading rate reinforces the idea that it is possible to understand a passage without necessarily reading every word, one word at a time. That is a very difficult habit to break, and many students balk at skipping words. They often say, "That's not *really reading*." (It is important to remember that reading word by word may be more than just a habit. It often reflects a student's cultural understanding about the nature and purpose of reading.)

Secondly, in academic settings which require reading in English, one of the most difficult challenges students face is the sheer magnitude of their reading assignments. ESL/EFL students who do not learn to read faster can spend three to four times longer than their native English-speaking classmates on completing the reading for a course. Then they have little time left over for thinking over and synthesizing the ideas they have learned from their reading.

Most importantly, reading rate affects comprehension. Research shows that the short-term memory will not hold information for more than a few seconds. The reader needs to take in enough of the text at one time to allow the brain to make sense of it. The brain cannot do its work effectively unless students learn to read at a rate of about 200 words per minute (Smith 1982). Therefore, improved comprehension will result from learning to read faster.

It is a good idea to teach reading rate improvement techniques and provide practice in class two or three times a week, and, if possible, to assign additional practice in the reading lab or at home. In class, students should read materials at their English language proficiency level "against the clock" and then answer comprehension check questions. Once they get into the routine, students enjoy seeing their own progress, especially if they use a graph such as the one that follows for keeping a record of their rate and comprehension.

Materials for Practicing Reading Rate Improvement

Reading rate improvement materials should not be too difficult for the student. In most classes, this means that the students will not all work on the same materials for practicing faster reading. Furthermore, students usually have a wide range of reading rates. It makes sense, then, to individualize reading rate improvement practice, assigning appropriate materials to each student to work on at their own pace. For these reasons, the materials used for practicing faster reading will usually not be the basis for other lessons or for class discussions.

There is another reason for using rate-building materials strictly for that purpose, and not, for example, for comprehension skills or intensive reading lessons. The students need to feel free to risk experimenting with the rate-building strategies as they work on the practice materials. When students know that they will "be accountable" in a serious way for what they are reading (more than privately checking their own comprehension), they slow down, and their reading habits will not change very much.

Some of the materials for reading rate improvement described here were not designed especially for ESL/EFL or other limited English proficient students. These materials often lack illustrations which can help the reader establish context, and they often assume cultural background knowledge. But they do provide interesting practice passages at multiple proficiency levels and

Progress Chart for Faster Reading
1 – 20

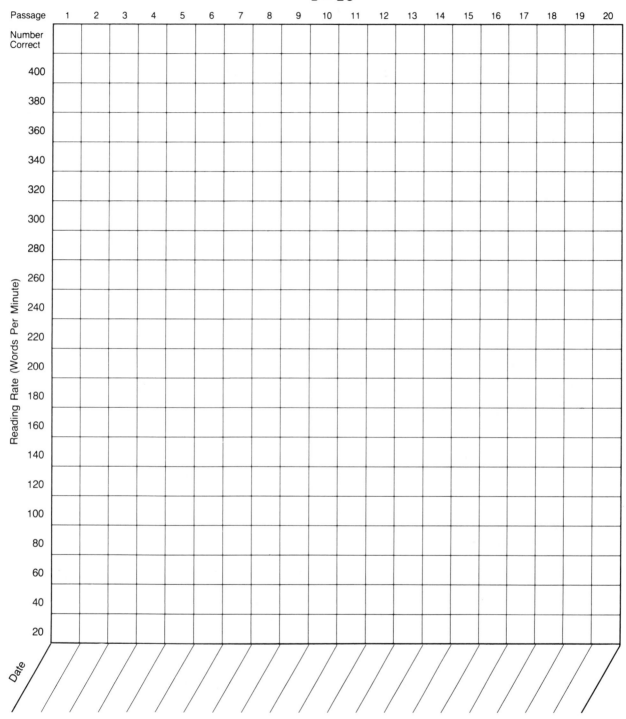

they are conveniently packaged with answer keys, making them suitable for independent, individualized use by the students.

Teachers who have never taught reading rate improvement will appreciate the *Timed Readings* series by Spargo and Williston (1980), because at the front of each book they will find thirteen pages of instructions and guidelines for improving reading rate. This information is very helpful to the teacher.

The *Timed Readings* series consists of books at ten reading ability levels, ranging from United States grade four to college level. The fifty 400-word passages in each book are followed by ten questions, five literal and five interpretative. A sample passage from Book 5 (with questions) follows.

32. Handiwork of the Gods

| Reading Time _____ |
| Comprehension Score _____ |
| Words per Minute _____ |

Early men, knowing only that the moon was a strange but regular visitor to their night skies, included its phases in their calendars as measurements of time. But the moon was thought to be the handiwork of the gods. Its origin was hidden in myths.

As truth replaced mythology, fact replaced mystery. Steadily, man's understanding of the moon grew as he began to develop instruments and methods for studying the earth's nearest neighbor.

There have been many contributions along this long road of progress. A few milestones stand out as tributes to human cleverness.

Galileo, in 1609, was one of the first to use the telescope in the study of heavenly bodies. In addition to viewing the features on the surface of the moon, he saw that Jupiter also had moons. He saw that many planets had moon-like phases. This last point supported the highly disputed Copernican theory that the sun, not the earth, was the center of the solar system.

In 1864 a camera was mounted on a telescope and the first photographs of the moon were obtained. Since then many new methods and devices for studying the moon have been developed. Powerful telescopes, infrared photography, and radar and laser beams have provided much information about the nature of the moon's surface. With such modern equipment the moon can be brought to a viewing distance of 400 miles from the earth. But until the space age, all methods of viewing and studying the moon were earthbound, and lunar features smaller than 1,500 feet in diameter could not be clearly seen.

The nation's effort to land men on the moon added to the need for a better understanding of the nature of the lunar surface. Unmanned spacecraft, sent to the moon to photograph its surface at close range, transmitted closeup pictures of features never before seen.

On July 31, 1964, Ranger VII made a successful flight to the moon. It crashed on the Ocean of Storms. But during the last few minutes of flight, its television cameras transmitted thousands of pictures back to earth. Lunar features as small as three feet in diameter could be clearly seen.

On July 2, 1966, Surveyor I soft-landed on the moon. Shortly after landing, its television camera began transmitting photographs. Pits and grains that measured fractions of an inch in diameter were easily seen in the televised photos.

Selection 32: Recalling Facts

1. Galileo lived during the early
   - ☐ a. 1500s.
   - ☐ b. 1600s.
   - ☐ c. 1700s.

2. Galileo's work supported the theories of
   - ☐ a. Plato.
   - ☐ b. Socrates.
   - ☐ c. Copernicus.

3. The first telescopic pictures of the moon were taken during
   - ☐ a. the middle 1800s.
   - ☐ b. the late 1800s.
   - ☐ c. the early 1900s.

4. The best telescopes bring the moon to a viewing distance of
   - ☐ a. 50 miles.
   - ☐ b. 200 Miles.
   - ☐ c. 400 miles.

5. The first space vehicle to make a soft landing on the moon was
   - ☐ a. Ranger VII.
   - ☐ b. Surveyor I.
   - ☐ c. Gemini II.

Selection 32: Understanding Ideas

6 The article is developed with
   - ☐ a. historical facts.
   - ☐ b. personal interviews.
   - ☐ c. general opinions.

7. Galileo is credited with the discovery of
   - ☐ a. Jupiter's moons.
   - ☐ b. Saturn's rings.
   - ☐ c. Mars' canals.

8. According to the article, some early astronomers believed that
   - ☐ a. the moon was another planet.
   - ☐ b. the earth was the center of the solar system.
   - ☐ c. the earth was flat.

9. In this article the author fails to mention that
   - ☐ a. laser beams are used to detect features on the moon's surface.
   - ☐ b. radar is used in lunar research.
   - ☐ c. men have walked on the moon.

10. The title of this article, "Handiwork of the Gods," refers to
   - ☐ a. religious sentiment surrounding the creation of the universe.
   - ☐ b. scientists' views of man.
   - ☐ c. early man's idea of the moon.

   (from *Timed Readings*)

The Jamestown *Timed Readings* are set up so that the individual students can learn to time themselves, answer the questions, check the answers, and record their progress on their own. This promotes independence and self-monitoring. Most students enjoy trying to break their own speed record.

Another popular book for practicing reading rate improvement is Fry's *Reading Drills for Speed and Comprehension* (1978). Each chapter contains interesting readings at three levels (easy, average, and difficult), followed by multiple-choice questions, cloze tests, and a vocabulary check. The section on how to use the book is very helpful for teachers who have not taught rate improvement before. Students seem to enjoy this book because of the interesting topics, the inclusion of three difficulty levels to choose from, and the variety of comprehension checks.

One of the oldest stand-bys for rate improvement work is the kit, *Rate Builders* (Parker 1973), an example of which was shown on page 53. This set contains 150 reading cards at ten reading levels. Each card, including comprehension questions, is designed to be read in the same amount of time, with the entire class timed simultaneously by the teacher, although each student may be working at a different level. The intention is that as students advance to longer passages with more questions, their reading rate will gradually increase.

This approach is not always popular with students. They often prefer to be actively engaged in reading against the clock and independently calculating their reading rate in words per minute, rather than having the instructor time them. In addition, many of the Rate Builder cards assume prior cultural knowledge which may not be known by ESL/EFL and other non-"mainstream" students. Also, Rate Builder cards often provide very short passages.

For the high-beginning-level students, two books which include passages for practice in reading rate improvement are: *Time and Space: A Basic Reader* (Connelly and Sims 1982) and *Reading Power* (Mikulecky and Jeffries 1986).

Another way to promote reading rate improvement is to teach students to use their own pleasure reading books for "reading against the clock." If they keep a record of their rate each day, they almost always show an increase. (This is due to the student's adaptation to the style and lexicon of the author of the book and the build-up of contextual knowledge as the students "get into" the book.) The chart below can be used to show students how to compute words per page and then keep a daily record of their reading rate.

Finding Your Reading Rate in Your Own Book

Book Title _____

1. Find out how many words are on one page of your book.
   a. Find a page in your book which is full from top to bottom.

      Count the number of words in three lines. _____

   b. Divide that number by three to find the average. _____

   c. Count the number of lines on one page. _____

   d. Multiply:

   _____ × _____ = _____
   (Number of lines)   (Words in one line)   (Words on page)

2. Now that you know how many words are on one page in your book, you can find out how many words you read.

   a. Write the time here: _____

   b. Read 3 pages of your book.

   c. Write the time here: _____

   d. How many minutes did you read? _____

   e. Multiply:

   _____ × _____ = _____
   (Number of pages)   (Number of words   (Number of words
                            on one page)   you read)

3. Now you can find your reading rate (Words Per Minute). Divide the number of words you read (in 2.e.) by the number of minutes (in 2.d).

Reading for Pleasure Progress Chart

Book Title _____

Author _____

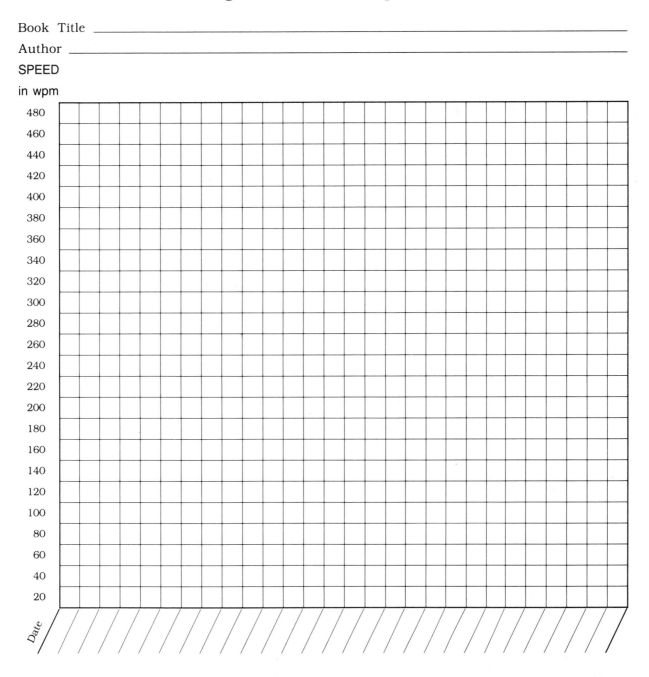

SPEED
in wpm

Techniques for Teaching Reading Rate Improvement

Sample Rationale

Most students read very slowly, especially in a second language. But research shows that you will not understand if you read slowly. Your brain needs to receive many ideas quickly in order to make sense of what you are reading. Reading faster is a skill that you can learn, just like running faster. It takes practice and some training from the "coach." We will work on reading faster in our class, and many students will be able to read twice as fast by the end of the semester.

1. Placement at appropriate levels. Students must be able to understand their rate building materials. It makes no sense to assign passages which are too difficult.

SRA *Rate Builders* are accompanied by a placement test, which makes it easy to assign the students at the proper level. The Jamestown *Timed Readings* and other books mentioned above include no such placement test, and so the levels must be assigned informally. For example, for the Jamestown books, cloze tests can be devised from several passages from level 5, the middle of the series. Students can select the cloze passage they wish to read, so that topic interest is not a major factor in their scores.

Students who read the Book 5 passage at a passing level (33–38% correct, exact word scoring) can be assigned to that level. The levels for students scoring higher or lower can be extrapolated from there. In an intensive ESL program (university level), the following chart was developed for assigning the *Timed Readings* books based on this informal testing procedure.

Cloze Score (exact word)	Book Number
0–15%	1
15–20%	2
20–28%	3
28–33%	4
33–38%	5
38–43%	6
43–48%	7
48–53%	8
53–58%	9
58%–up	10

These correlations were made in 1982 and were used for four successive summers in a university setting. They worked out well. However, individual teachers should tailor such correlations to meet the needs of the students in their classes.

If a student is assigned to a level which is too difficult (unable to score above 60 per cent on subsequent comprehension check questions), that individual should be assigned to a lower level. But obviously, for self-esteem purposes, it is always better to estimate low and then have to *raise* a student to a *higher* level rather than the opposite.

2. This approach to teaching reading rate improvement strategies is based on using the Jamestown series. Reading rate lessons are all-class activities, even though the students are usually not all working on the same text. The procedures listed here are suggested ways for the teacher to act as the "coach" in the skill of reading faster.

a. Taking a base rate. Before any instruction takes place, the students should measure their initial reading rate. This is also an excellent time for them to learn how to time themselves and record their own progress on charts and graphs. (Record keeping is an important motivator and students should do this for themselves.)

It is a good idea to have all of the students do three "base rate" timed readings. Make sure there is a large clock with a second hand easily visible to the class. The students will all begin to read at the same moment, but they will all finish at different times. They need to be able to record exactly what time they finish reading a passage. *The questions are not timed.*

b. Setting goals. All students can improve their reading rate. In one semester, it is not unusual for many to double their reading speed. The class should discuss this after they have found their initial rates. Then they can set realistic goals for the semester.

c. Previewing. The first lesson in rate improvement should be about previewing before reading. Please refer to Part III. B. in this book for directions and a rationale for teaching the previewing skill.

d. "Swinging two bats," or "It feels so good when I slow down." This is a technique for making a fast speed feel comfortable.

- Ask all the students to turn to the next passage in their *Timed Readings* book, and tell them that this time you will time them, and they will have *one minute* to read the passage. Of course, this is three to five times faster than most of them can read. They will probably do poorly on the comprehension questions.

- But then tell them you will time them again, and this time they will have *two minutes* to read the next passage. The two minutes will seem like a long time for them.

- Ask the students to do one more timed reading, timing themselves. This third timing usually results in a higher rate than they have had before.

e. Pacing exercises. In the *Timed Readings* books, small dots are printed in the right-hand margin of the passages, spaced at every 100 words. The teacher can help students learn to read faster by doing pacing exercises. A reasonable time limit can be selected, i.e., 125 words per minute. As the students read, the teacher taps on the table periodically. At each tap, the students should move their eyes down the page to the next black dot in the margin.

f. Recording progress. Although there is much to be said in favor of a graph for recording reading rate progress, (for example, the graph shown on page 59) teachers might want to consider using a progress chart instead. The chart shown below is effective because in addition to quantitative information, students can record the titles of the passages and their comments about their own performance. They can give reasons for their reading rate and comprehension scores (for example, unfamiliar/familiar topic; noise in classroom; feeling good today; interesting/uninteresting topic). Such record-keeping builds motivation because it provides concrete evidence of progress.

READING RATE PROGRESS CHART					
Name _____ Book No. _____					
Date	Chapter	Title	Rate	Comprehension	Comments

Whatever record-keeping system is used, be sure to circulate around the classroom while the students are recording their scores, briefly discuss the results with each student, and ask for reasons for variations in rate.

When reading rate improvement exercises become a regular part of the reading class, even at the beginning level, students *do* learn to read faster, and they also learn to vary their reading rate, depending on what they already know about the topic of the passage and their purpose for reading it.

D. IMPROVING BOTTOM-UP PROCESSING

We have stressed so far that many students, especially ESL/EFL students, rely excessively on bottom-up processing, primarily at the word and sentence level, when they read. Researchers (i.e. Coady 1979) have stressed the need for training students in top-down, conceptually-driven processing. Coady (1979:11) states:

> The teacher should always put primary emphasis in reading instruction on comprehension strategies . . . In short, too much emphasis on concrete process strategies such as letter-sound correspondences can leave the student with a poor priority of strategies.

However Mackay, in the same volume (1979:81), states:

> To ask a student to demonstrate a skill may indicate whether or not he has mastered it, but it may teach the student nothing. If our purpose is not to *test* but to *teach*, then our materials should provide the student with linguistic information about how a text conveys meaning, so that he can use the information in order to understand not only the text under scrutiny, but any text his studies may require him to cope with.

According to Mackay, linguistic information includes:

1. The spelling system of English
   (Knowing which letters can and cannot follow others.)

2. The grammatical system of English
   (Knowing which words can and cannot be placed in certain parts of the sentence.)

3. Semantic knowledge
   (Knowing which words are or are not appropriate in certain contexts.)
4. Textual grammar in English
   (Knowing the linguistic features which tie a series of statements together to form a text.)

Recent research would seem to support Mackay. Stoller (1986) cites studies which show that the teaching of some bottom-up skills is necessary, especially for beginning level students and for students whose native language does not use the Roman alphabet.

In fact, when students read a second language, they will compensate for a lack of topic information by relying on word level clues to meaning (Stanovich 1981). The problem is that they may unconsciously and mistakenly rely on language features which function as clues to meaning in their native language, but not in English (Cziko 1978).

In order to promote the development of fluent, effective reading, it is a good idea for students to learn and practice some of the bottom-up strategies which good readers employ. Research has shown that good native speaker readers unconciously engage in a great many perceptual processes when they read (Haber and Haber 1981). These automatic processes include the ability to recognize letters and words on sight; identify a form or a syntactic structure at a glance; recognize and unconsciously apply redunduncies in English.

With effective instruction and practice in the ways that meaning is conveyed by such linguistic features as spelling, vocabulary, and grammar, ESL/EFL and other limited English proficient students can learn to sample a text more effectively. This would allow more processing time for the application of conceptual frameworks (top-down processing) (Eskey 1986:8).

Perceptual Skills

Haber and Haber (1981) point out that good native speaker readers unconsciously perceive and recognize such aspects of text as letter shapes and common words. Stoller (1986) and others argue that visual discrimination training is essential for ESL/EFL readers. She states (1986:56):

> The word and phrase recognition exercises are intended to help students develop their so-called 'bottom-up' skills. That is, students learn to react rapidly and accurately to the appearance of English words and then English phrases as a whole. From these activities, students develop a sense of the visual image of key words and phrases.

In this section, sample exercises for this skill will be presented. Some of these, modeled after Stoller (1986) and Harris (1966), are intended exclusively for visual discrimination practice. Meaning and pronunciation of the lexical items are temporarily ignored.

As Stoller states (1986:56–57):

> These recognition exercises are not to be mistaken as actual 'readings', nor are they to be confused with vocabulary enrichment exercises. They are simply recognition exercises, sometimes referred to as perception or identification exercises, one of the first crucial steps in a reading skills development program.

Additional exercises are included which combine visual perception training with vocabulary reinforcement and comprehension development.

Sample Rationale

Your eyes and your brain know the letters, words, and phrases of your native language automatically. You can recognize them without even thinking, and that helps you to read in your native language. But English is new to you. If you want to read and think in English, your eyes and brain need to learn to recognize English letters, words, and phrases automatically, too. We will work on some exercises to help you read better and faster in English.

Identification Exercises

These exercises should always be strictly timed.

Sample Exercise D.1.

Directions: The teacher will time you very strictly. In each line of words, one word is different from all of the others. Scan each line and circle the word that is different.

Example: our our own our our.
WORK FAST!

1. new	new	new	now	new
2. is	in	is	is	is
3. my	my	by	my	my
4. me	me	me	we	me
5. our	one	one	one	one
6. him	him	him	him	his
7. had	had	did	had	had
8. may	may	my	may	may
9. there	these	there	there	there
10. when	then	when	when	when
11. her	has	has	has	has
12. now	own	now	now	now
13. your	your	your	year	your
14. then	them	them	them	them
15. with	will	with	with	with
16. That	That	That	That	Than
17. much	much	most	much	much
18. out	out	out	not	out
19. is	is	is	is	it
20. yours	years	years	years	years

Sample Exercise D.2.

The key words in this exercise are small but important. About half of every page you read in English is made up of words like these.

Directions: Work at top speed. Read the key word and then scan the line. Circle the key word every time you see it.

Starting time ⎯⎯⎯⎯⎯⎯⎯⎯⎯⎯⎯⎯

1. into	onto	unto	until	into	intro	into
2. been	been	bean	born	been	bane	been
3. back	black	bark	back	back	book	both
4. must	much	must	mist	must	mash	muse
5. then	them	then	thin	then	their	then
6. way	way	why	wax	way	way	wry
7. out	our	cut	oust	out	our	out
8. all	all	ail	aim	all	owe	alm
9. with	witch	with	wish	sill	with	wilt
10. over	ever	over	aver	our	out	over
11. they	thy	they	then	thirty	them	they
12. what	what	which	what	when	what	white
13. down	dawn	darn	done	down	dean	down
14. may	may	my	many	way	may	marry
15. time	turn	twon	time	twine	time	tine
16. would	want	would	could	should	would	world
17. you	you	yes	yon	you	your	yore
18. also	alas	alto	also	alter	also	ails
19. much	must	mast	must	much	munch	mulch
20. after	alter	altar	afar	after	otter	after

Finishing time ⎯⎯⎯⎯⎯⎯⎯⎯⎯⎯⎯⎯

Sample Exercise D.3.

Directions: Read the key phrase. Scan and circle the key phrase every time you see it. Work at top speed.

Starting time: ⎯⎯⎯⎯⎯⎯⎯⎯⎯⎯⎯⎯

A. Key phrase: after class

after math . . . . . after class . . . . . under class . . . . . after class . . . . .
other class . . . . . mother's class . . . . . after closing . . . . . math class
. . . . . after class . . . . . other math . . . . . after class . . . . . after the course
. . . . . . under course . . . . . after class.

B. Key phrase: <u>rent a movie</u>

sent a movie . . . . . rent a car . . . . . sent a note . . . . . rent a movie . . . . . rent a tape . . . . . sent a movie . . . . . like a movie . . . . . rest a while . . . . . rent a van . . . . . . rent a movie.

C. Key phrase: <u>across the street</u>

across the road . . . . across the aisle . . . . . under the street . . . . across the street . . . . . across the screen . . . . . across the bridge . . . . . acorns in trees . . . . . across the street . . . . . after the treat . . . . . across the street.

Finishing time _____

Perceptual Training Combined with Meaningful Text

Sample Exercise D.4.

Directions: Work at top speed. The key words in this exercise are taken from the story we read in class about acupuncture. The first word in each line is the key word. Scan the line, and circle the key word each time you see it.

Note: This is a fictitious class. You would use the words and topics which your own students have discussed in class.

Starting time:_____

<u>doctors</u>	doctors	directors	doctors	dentists
<u>soaked</u>	socked	soaked	soaks	sealed
<u>small</u>	snail	small	small	smell
<u>being</u>	buying	boring	being	betting
<u>needle</u>	noodle	needle	normal	needle
<u>pain</u>	pane	pine	paint	pain
<u>specialist</u>	sportsman	specialist	spicier	special
<u>decade</u>	decide	decorate	denied	decade
<u>ailments</u>	airports	asthma	ailments	alleyways
<u>backaches</u>	bookmarks	backpacks	backaches	backwards

Finishing time: _____

Word visualization and recognition ability can also be enhanced by using a popular game-like reading activity called the Word Search Puzzle. Examples of word search puzzles may be found in small booklets of puzzles for sale at local book stores and supermarket check-out counters in many parts of the United States (i.e., *Variety Word Find Puzzles* 1988) and the idea is used occasionally in second language texts, too (i.e., Motta and Riley 1984).

Word search puzzles can reinforce the language learners' perception of letters and words in English, as well as the spelling of words. They can also be used to reinforce spelling and the spelling *rules* of English when false "almost" words are included.

A typical word search puzzle is shown here. Notice that the puzzle can also reinforce students' knowledge of semantic categories; in this puzzle, all of the words to find are in the category of family members.

Sample Exercise D.5.

WORD SEARCH PUZZLE
The Family

Directions: Find and circle the hidden words in the puzzle. Some are hidden across, some are up and down, and some are at an angle.

father   grandson   aunt   daughter   mother   uncle

```
d  f  n  o  c  w  d  y  a  e  l  k
i  a  a  o  l  d  n  a  l  r  m  t
s  t  u  f  e  m  n  c  v  c  x  z
i  h  n  g  r  a  n  d  s  o  n  v
w  e  t  r  h  u  j  l  m  i  b  b
p  r  a  t  h  t  r  c  r  i  n  z
r  e  h  p  o  q  e  r  t  l  c  w
m  o  t  h  e  r  h  r  m  c  v  x
```

Teachers can devise word search puzzles for reviewing vocabulary or for introducing new words within a category. The puzzles are very simple to construct, and students may enjoy devising them for each other. The following puzzle is from *Impact!*, a beginning level literacy text for adults. The students had already read a short passage containing the words in the puzzle, which was planned as a take-home supplementary acitivty (Motta and Riley 1984).

The Apartment Building

here	playing	young
grandmother	it	four
apartment	now	he's
landlord	renting	above
studying	student	
divorced	it's	

Directions: Find the words. Circle them.

```
f  e  m  n  b  v  c  x  z  l  k  j
t  m  r  l  a  n  d  l  o  r  d  i
r  i  t' s  s  r  e  n  t  i  n  g
s  s  t  u  d  y  i  n  g  g  i  t
i  a  b  o  v  e  m (h  e  r  e) i
g  r  a  n  d  m  o  t  h  e  r  h
q  q  w  r  e  u  v  y  o  u  n  g
s  a  f  o  u  r  i  o  h  e' s  h
f  d  h  g  d  i  v  o  r  c  e  d
p  o  i  u  y  s  t  u  d  e  n  t
b  v  a  p  a  r  t  m  e  n  t  a
p  l  a  y  i  n  g  l  r  n  o  w
s  d  f  h  k  i  p  e  m  u  b  t
```

(from *Impact! Book 1 Teacher's Guide*)

Word search puzzles can also be assigned with no word list provided. You can tell the students what the category is, and then they can try to find a given number of words which fit that category. This can be varied according to the vocabulary knowledge of the students.

Another exercise for training students in word perception in a meaningful context is shown below. The lower half of every word is missing. The students are to read the passage, mentally supplying the missing halves of the letters. (Modeled after Haber and Haber 1981.)

Sample Exercise D.6.

Directions: As you read this passage, you will find that you can understand the story and answer the True-False questions even if only half of each letter is printed. Your brain makes up the other half!

A car thief at Boston's Logan International Airport got more than he expected last night. The car he stole was not empty: A two-year-old girl and two poodle dogs were asleep in the back seat. Greg Winter, the child's father, left the car outside the terminal, in order to run in to bring his wife, Susan, a sandwich. Susan works for a car rental agency in the main terminal.

Imagine Winter's dismay when he came out to find his car gone! He called the police and then he went with them to search the near-by streets. The car (with child and dogs safe inside) was found in less than two hours. The thief, apparently recognizing his mistake, had abandoned the car in East Boston.

Questions: True or False?

1. Three children were in the car.   T F
2. The father was at work that day.   T F
3. The car was found in East Boston.   T F
4. The mother works for a car rental agency.   T F

Automatic Decoding

Decoding — recognizing and identifying words — is one of the processes which good native speaker readers do automatically with large portions of a text (Haber and Haber 1981). For example, Haber and Haber list 100 commonly-used words which good native speaker readers identify automatically. It is interesting to note that these words make up about 50% of every printed page in English.

a   I   in   an   to   of   is   we   he   it   as   no   be   on   so   do   if   or   me
by   my   up   was   new   are   now   one   our   can   man   for   his   her
him   has   two   she   who   its   and   not   out   but   did   had   the   all
you   may   any   was   were   from   said   this   when   that   more   have
such   than   also   with   will   what   some   been   most   them   over   time
must   then   even   down   much   what   into   made   like   back   they
your   only   many   before   through   which   about   there   their   these
would   could   after   first   years   where

(Carroll, Davies and Richman 1971, cited in Haber and Haber 1981:174.)

Automatic recognition of these words makes comprehension of the text easier because it allows the reader to use more of the limited capacity of the eye-brain information processing system for attending to other aspects of the text and for making connections with prior knowledge (Stanovich 1980). Some teachers, therefore, may be tempted to teach the words directly, perhaps by using flash cards and other drill methods. That might seem like the logical thing to do, but research has shown that such approaches are not as effective as teaching these common words in meaningful contexts.

For instance, Fleisher, Jenkins, and Pany (1979) found that:

Lack of automaticity may limit comprehension because too much mental effort is devoted to decoding. However, research has shown that 'short-term instruction on isolated words is not adequate to affect comprehension and speeded practice needs to focus on words in context instead.' (Cited in Beck and McKeown 1986:117.)

One way to help students develop automatic identification is to assign cloze-type exercises in which the *outlines* of the words are shown, but not the actual letters. Such exercises can be aided (hidden words given in a list) or unaided (hidden words not given), depending on the needs of the students. The following exercise is modeled after Haber and Haber (1981:173).

Sample Exercise D.7.

Directions: These words are hidden in the story.

a	was	and	about	to	the
But	about	could	not	This	she
of	She	this			

Read the story, and use the shapes to guess the words. Write the words under the shapes. Work with another student.

Helen Keller

Helen Keller was ▮ famous American. She ▬▬ writer ▬▬ speaker. ▬ wrote books ▬ articles ▬▬ education ▬ politics. ▬ traveled ▮ every part ▬ ▬ world. ▬ ▬ suprising fact ▬▬ Helen Keller is ▬: ▬ ▬ ▬ see ▬ ▬ ▬ hear. ▬ blind, deaf woman ▬▮ very special person.

(Adapted from *Reading Power*)

Spelling, Grammar, and Reading

Although English classes usually deal with spelling, grammar, and word meanings, students may not be aware that knowledge of these linguistic features can improve their reading skill. This lack of awareness is especially likely if the instruction is rule-based (e.g., rote learning) rather than meaning based (e.g., contextualized exercises based on an explicit rationale).

An extreme example of a rule-based approach to teaching spelling which makes no explicit connection to comprehension would be something like this:

Rule: In order to add the suffix *-ing* to verbs which end with *-e*, it is necessary to drop the *-e*.

Exercise: Here is a list of verbs which end in *-e*. Notice that you drop the final *-e* before adding *-ing*.

> come   coming
> have
> make
> bake
> smile

Examples of such rule-based, out-of-context spelling lessons, word analysis exercises and word-form tasks abound in commercially produced language skills texts. There are other ways to teach. The lessons in this section are examples of meaning-based practice for developing a greater awareness of some of the lexical and grammatical features which are especially useful for improving reading. The idea is that the more textual clues to meaning that the reader can take note of, the more rapid and accurate the reading will be.

A cloze activity which reinforces spelling skills is the C-test, developed by Raatz and Klein-Braley (1984). "Every second word is deleted. However, in order to ensure that solution is possible at all, we leave the first half of the deleted word standing. If the word has an odd number of letters, we delete exactly half the word plus half a letter. If the word consists only of one letter, then this word is ignored in the counting, and half the following word is deleted . . . . . Only entirely correct restorations are counted as right."

This exercise develops bottom-up skills because it focuses on the words in the text, and cues the first half of the missing words. This English C-test, Senior Version, is excerpted from Raatz and Klein-Braley (1984).

Sample Exercise D.8.

Directions: In this story, parts of many words are missing. Using the story to help you, write the missing parts on the lines.

"The evening of October 30, 1938, was just like any other quiet Sunday

night to most of the people of America. Many fami_ _ _ _ were a_ home

rea_ _ _ _ the pap_ _ or conte_ _ _ _ _ _ listening t_ the rad_ _. There

we_ _ two prog_ _ _ _ that nig_ _ which attr_ _ _ _ _ large audi_ _ _ _ _.

One w_ _ the pl_ _ produced b_ Orson Welles. T_ _ listeners prep_ _ _ _

themselves f_ _ an ho_ _ of comfo_ _ _ _ _ _ excitement, be_ _ after th_

opening announ_ _ _ _ _ _, the pl_ _ did n_ _ start. Instead there was dance

music."

Cloze exercises are effective for making students aware of how specific linguistic knowledge facilitates reading. Deletions of grammatical categories can heighten the learners' awareness of the importance of grammatical knowledge for skilled reading. For example, given a text which has all of the prepositions deleted, the students will learn about the functions of prepositions in understanding a text in English. Sets of directions or recipes work especially well for this kind of exercise.

A classic example is "How to Make a Peanut Butter Sandwich" with all of the prepositions removed and listed on the bottom of the page. Students first read the recipe and write in the blanks what they think are the correct prepositions. Then teams of students, armed with bread, peanut butter, and knives, attempt to follow the directions *to the letter*. A mistake may mean spreading the peanut butter *under* the bread.

In order to call attention to the importance of punctuation as clues to meaning and to develop the language learner's awareness of syntax, a passage with all the punctuation removed is effective (Grellet 1981). As students work together on such a passage, they predict where sentences are likely to stop, based on the *meaning* of the passage.

Sample Exercise D.9.

Directions: Working in pairs, decide where the punctuation should go. Compare your results with another pair of students. Explain the reasons for your punctuation.

The Lion and The Mouse

One day a mouse ran over the tail of a lion that was sleeping in the middle of the path the lion awoke with a start and became very angry at being awakened he caught the mouse with his great paws and put the mouse in his mouth the mouse shouted oh please do not eat me if you let me go maybe i can help you some day oh please mr lion let me go and the mouse cried and cried the lion laughed loud to hear the tiny mouse say he could help him some day but he let him go because he was so amused one day a few weeks later the mouse found a lion caught in a great rope net the lion was roaring fiercely and trying to get out but he was trapped in the net and the more he struggled the more he was caught the little mouse peered into the net and saw that it was his old friend the lion he remembered the lion's kindness he gnawed the net he worked all afternoon finally there was a hole for the lion to crawl through the lion said even little friends can be big friends

E. WORD KNOWLEDGE FOR SKILLED READING

Obviously, an entire book could be devoted to this subject. In this chapter, sample lessons, guidelines, and suggestions based on recent first and second language reading research will be summarized, including interesting sources for further reading about vocabulary development.

First, teachers should remember that, compared to native speakers, the vocabularies of their ESL/EFL and limited English proficient students are very small. For example, Crow and Quigley (1985) point out that a native speaker of English has acquired approximately 150,000 words by the age of 18. They remark that if ESL/EFL students learned 40 lexical units every day for four years, they still would not match the vocabulary of the native speaker!

Research has shown (Freebody and Anderson 1983; Hall, White, and Guthrie 1986) the close relationship between vocabulary development and skilled reading, although other researchers question the *causal* nature of that relationship (Tierney and Cunningham 1984). Nevertheless, most teachers of reading consider vocabulary development as part of their job. But which words to teach and how to teach them?

For enhancing reading comprehension, the key vocabulary items are often *not the content words but the function words* (Cooper 1984) which serve as cohesion devices, tying the text together and signaling the relationships between concepts and ideas. These function words, an essential component of vocabulary development for skilled reading, include pronouns, synonyms, hyponyms, summary words, and the lexical items which signal the relationship between ideas in a text (i.e., however, then, also).

Of course, content words are not unimportant. Consequently, this part of the book has been divided into two sections. Section 1 includes sample exercises which can help students acquire some of the function words mentioned above. Section 2 offers ideas for methods of teaching content words.

Function Words

Pronouns

Pronouns are the most widely-used of all the cohesion devices. They present a double problem for second language students: "local" meaning within sentences and text-level meaning as signals of connections between parts of a text.

Lessons on the use of pronouns for reading improvement may represent a new way of thinking about pronouns for some teachers, whose usual practice is to teach pronouns from a strictly grammatical point of view. But it can also be effective to teach the pronouns and their functions as devices of textual cohesion within a meaningful context.

Sample Rationale

Writers do not like to use the same word many times. They often use other words which mean almost the same thing.

Sometimes pronouns are used instead of nouns. They are small words, but they are very important when you are reading. You will understand more if you pay attention to pronouns.

he	she	it	they	we	you
I	them	him	her	these	those

In these examples, the pronouns are underlined:

EXAMPLE A

Mary Simms lives in New York City. <u>She</u> has an apartment near Central Park. Mary jogs in the park. <u>She</u> thinks that jogging is good for <u>her</u>. So <u>she</u> jogs three times a week.

All the underlined pronouns take the place of the noun, Mary Simms. "Mary Simms" is called the referent.

EXAMPLE B

Jogging is good for your health for a few reasons. <u>It</u> is especially good for your heart. If you do <u>it</u> a few days a week, your heart will be stronger. <u>It</u> is also good for your legs. And many people believe <u>it</u> is good for your mind.

All of the underlined pronouns take the place of the noun _____
_____ is the referent.

Sample Exercise E.1. Beginning Level

In these sentences, the pronouns are underlined. Circle the referents.

1. Running is not a new sport. People were doing it hundreds of years ago.
2. Runners know that a good diet is important. They eat very healthy foods, especially before a race.
3. Every year, there are many long races in many parts of the world. Sports fans watch them on television.
4. The Boston race is called the Boston Marathon. This is one of the oldest races in the United States.
5. In some races, the winners get large amounts of money. But for almost 100 years, they got no money at all in the Boston race.
6. In 1985, more than 6,000 people ran in the Boston Marathon. They came from all over the world.

(from *Reading Power*)

Sample Exercise E.2. Advanced Level

Directions: Some of the pronouns in this passage are underlined. As you read the passage, draw an arrow from each of these pronouns to its referent. Then write a list of the pronouns and their referents on a sheet of paper. Work with another student.

The Ensemble

The best plays are created by a "tight ensemble." This means that the actors know each other well and that they trust each other. They seek advice from one another and ask for feedback. They do not fear making "mistakes" in rehearsals. That is what rehearsals are for. The same situation is beneficial to a group of language learners. They should feel free to criticize one another in a constructive manner, and they should learn to enjoy experimenting with the new language in front of their peers.

Language teachers can foster this feeling by minimizing the inhibitions of their students. The most obvious approach is to avoid making students' inhibitions any worse than they already are. The language class, like the rehearsal, should be an atmosphere conducive to open experimentation with the second language. It is much easier to be open and relaxed in front of friends than strangers.

(Adapted from *The Theater Arts and the Teaching of Second Language*)

Synonyms

Students with limited vocabularies may mistakenly infer that two different things are mentioned in a text when, in fact, two words or phrases refer to the same thing. A series of exercises which focus on synonyms will bring this to the students' attention. After they have had some practice in recognizing the functions of synonyms in a text, they can use their knowledge as a strategy for sorting out passages which do not make sense to them.

Sample Rationale

One way that writers try to make their writing interesting and enjoyable to read is by not repeating the same words over and over. Instead, they may use a few different words to name the same thing. You can learn to read better if you learn to recognize synonyms in English.

Sample Exercise E.3. Advanced Level

Directions: Read the following sentences. Draw an arrow from the italicized word to the word or words that have the same meaning as the italicized word. Notice that sometimes you have to draw an arrow to a group of words. Also, notice that the meaning of a word may be repeated with words that have a different form (e.g., an adjective may be re-expressed in a noun form).

> *Example:* Henning found that students with a lower *proficiency* in English made more of their mistakes on words that sound alike. His results suggest that students with less skill in English hold the sound of words in their short-term memory.

Natural Resources

1. One of the *predominant* concerns today is the future of our natural resources. This issue is of greatest importance because it is becoming clear to many people that our present resources will not last forever.

2. Some people claim that twentieth-century man is using up resources at an increasing rate. The *acceleration* in *consumption* is partially a function of the steady improvement in the standard of living.

3. In some *isolated* regions in the world, people continue to live as they did years ago. In these areas which are separated from the rest of the country, there does not seem to be a great concern with conserving natural resources.

4. Should the government *regulate* the cost of resources such as oil and gas? Some people do not believe that government control is the solution to the problem of the rising cost of fuel.

5. The recent *data* on energy production in the United States indicate that the production of nuclear energy is increasing. The information also indicates that the production of hydroelectric power is decreasing.

6. Some groups of scientists are trying to *devise* systems that would allow us to use solar energy. If they can invent a functional system, perhaps we can become less dependent on fossil fuels such as oil and coal.

7. Suppose there were not enough iron to manufacture steel. The *scarcity* of iron would affect most of the heavy industries in the country, and the entire national economy would change.

8. Cleaning up waterways is an *enormous task*. The job is so large, in fact, that the government may not be able to save some of the rivers and lakes which have been polluted.

9. When phosphates, a pollutant, are emptied into a lake, algae grow very fast. When algae *flourish*, the water supply may be lost.

10. What about the forests in our country? Is the published information on the preservation of the forest areas *reliable*? Can we trust the information we read?

Amy L. Sonka, Skillful Reading: A Text and Workbook for Students of English as a Second Language, © 1981, p. 187. Reprinted by permission of Prentice-Hall, Inc., Englewood Cliffs, N.J.

Hyponyms

Hyponyms are synonyms which name members of the same category but at different levels of specificity. The hyponyms in this passage are underlined:

Jane was re-reading page 9, as the teacher had suggested. The page was very difficult for her. In fact, the whole chapter was almost impossible to understand. She took a break, sighed, and went back to her book. She wished that the teacher would assign easier reading materials.

Notice that there is a pattern in the use of hyponyms: Each succeeding hyponym is more general than the one preceding it. This is quite common in English, and it seems to fit in with the topic/comment order, in which new information is stated before old. In focused exercises, students can learn how to use such knowledge about hyponyms to improve their reading comprehension. As always, it is a good idea to encourage students to discover patterns such as the one for hyponyms, rather than giving them a rule at the outset.

Sample Exercise E.4. Beginning Level

Directions: All of the words in each group refer to the same thing, but some words are more general than others. On your paper, write the words in order, beginning with the most specific and ending with the most general. Work with a partner.

Example: The Rolling Stones
          Rock music groups
          Rock music
          Popular music
          Music

1. Mt. McKinley
   Alaskan mountain
   mountain
   snow-capped mountain

2. evergreen tree
   tree
   tall pine tree
   Mrs. Brown's tall pine tree

3. Mr. Kim's house on Beacon Street
   house on Beacon Street
   house
   house in Boston

4. Lassie
   mammal
   animal
   dog
   living thing

5. Los Angeles
   city on planet earth
   city in the United States
   city
   city in California

Sample Exercise E.5. Beginning Level

Directions: A word is underlined in the first sentence of each passage. Circle the word or words in the next sentence which mean almost the same thing as the underlined word. Work with another student.

1. Liz moved to <u>Paris</u> last month. She likes the city very much.
2. Hiroko plays the <u>violin</u> in the Tokyo Symphony Orchestra. The sound of this stringed instrument is sweet and pure.
3. The <u>president of the city council</u> gave a long speech. As the leader, she has to plan many new projects.
4. The <u>tornado</u> hit a small town in Texas. The storm swept down the main street three times, and the terrible winds destroyed most of the town.
5. <u>Lemons, oranges and limes</u> are all very good to eat. These citrus fruits are also very healthy for you because they are a good source of vitamin C.

Write the hyponyms for each passage in order, from specific to general. The first one is done.

1. Paris, city

2.

3.

4.

5.

Note: Many ESL/EFL and other English textbooks include one or two exercises similar to those above, and it may be possible to find enough such exercises from several sources to be able to develop a sequence of lessons. But it is usually more effective to write your own, and it is not difficult, using passages from the newspaper or from a class text. In fact, students also enjoy designing these exercises themselves, using a textbook from another course and locating and analyzing the cohesion devices in passages of their choice.

Identifying Cohesion Devices

After students have worked with several types of cohesion devices, it is a good idea to ask them to apply their new knowledge to a longer text.

Sample Exercise E.6. Advanced Level

Directions: Writing is tied together by short, unimportant-looking words. But these little words are very important for understanding. Read this passage. Then go back and find the words and phrases listed below. Write the referents in the table. Work with another student.

The Effects of Dumping Hazardous Wastes

(1) In recent years, concern about the environment has grown as the public has become more aware of many common, dangerous dumping practices. (2) These practices, some of which have been going on for years, have increased as the population has grown. (3) Recent publicity has drawn public attention to one form of environmental pollution — the dumping of hazardous chemical wastes.

(4) These wastes include heavy metals and other by-products of technology. (5) Such chemicals often cause cancer, brain damage, and high infant mortality rates.

(6) Dumping of the wastes is difficult to monitor, and quite often even careful dumping has resulted in the destruction of whole areas. (7) When the wastes are first put into a dump, they are usually sealed in large metal drums. (8) As time passes, the metal rusts, and the waste materials begin to leak out into the surrounding soil. (9) This has two effects on the environment. (10) First, the local soil is often permanently destroyed and it must be removed. (11) It thus becomes additional hazardous waste to be stored somewhere else. (12) Second, the chemical waste can sink lower and lower into the soil and reach the water tables deep in the earth's surface. (13) The latter effect produces pollution of the water sources for many miles around. (14) In cases where the wastes leach into a river bed, they can be carried to one of the oceans, thus spreading the pollution globally.

(E. Mikulecky 1985, used by permission)

Sentence	Word or Words	Referents
1	these	
2	some of which	
4	these	
5	such chemicals	
7	they	
9	this	
10	it	
11	it	
13	the latter	

Summary Words

Collective nouns and other generalizing words are particularly challenging for ESL/EFL and other limited English proficient students because, as with other referents, they may not realize that one word is summarizing several others in a passage. For example, the word *process* in this passage.

> First, she boiled the water. Then she added a drop of vinegar and six eggs, and she let them boil for ten minutes. She placed the eggs in ice cold water for half an hour to cool them. Then she choped them and added them to the salad. The whole *process* took about an hour.

Such collective words are easy to teach if you begin by teaching hyponyms as described above. And because this kind of synonym requires thinking in terms of generalizations and examples, categorization exercises can be effective, too.

Sample Rationale

Writers often use a single word or phrase (a summary word) to tell about a whole collection of ideas or examples. You can improve your reading if you learn to recognize these summary words and phrases. They name a general idea in a passage which has many examples of that idea.

Sample Exercise E.7. Beginning Level

Directions: The words in each list are members of the same group. Write the name for each group. The first one is done. Work with another student.

1. SPORTS
   baseball
   basketball
   football
   swimming
   tennis

2. _____
   Mars
   Uranus
   Jupiter
   Saturn
   Mercury

3. _____
   Latin
   Greek
   Polish
   Chinese
   Farsi

4. _____
   malaria
   tuberculosis
   scarlet fever
   diptheria
   measles

5. _____
   cathedral
   church
   temple
   mosque
   chapel

6. _____
   television set
   VCR
   home computer
   phone answering machine

Sample Exercise E.8. Intermediate Level

Directions: In each short passage, the underlined word is a summary word which stands for several details in the passage. Below, write the summary words and then list the parts named in the passage. Work with another student.

1. The Flynn family's house was robbed last week. Robbers broke in while the family was out and stole a television set, a VCR, some jewelry, and their silver tea pot from France. The police are working on this case and they hope to recover the Flynn's <u>belongings.</u>

    Summary word:
    Parts:

2. Kilgore Trout's home library is well stocked. There are mystery books, novels, biographies, travel books, how-to manuals, science fiction thrillers, and reference books. This <u>collection</u> is the result of a life-long habit of reading for pleasure.

    Summary word:
    Parts:

3. Susan Diamond got her new SPEND credit card in the mail. She went shopping immediately. She bought groceries at the supermarket, shoes at the department store, and a set of new tires for her car at the auto supply store. She did not spend any money. The <u>purchases</u> were all made with her new credit card.

    Summary word:
    Parts:

4. For quite a long time, it has been known that sulfur dioxide is dangerous for people with sensitive respiratory systems. And some studies have shown a connection between increased levels of sulfur dioxiede in the air and large numbers of premature deaths. If the government does not stop the factories from polluting the air, many more <u>health problems</u> could arise.

    Summary words:
    Parts:

5. During the summer, the music in Massachusetts moves outdoors. Special concerts are performed in the Hatch Shell on the banks of the Charles River and in a special fenced-in part of Boston Common. The Boston Symphony Orchestra moves out to Tanglewood, an outdoor concert park in the Berkshire Mountains. Jazz, rock, classical, and big-band music can be enjoyed while sailing in Boston Harbor. These <u>musical events</u> help Bostonians forget the long, cold winter.

    Summary words:
    Parts:

Lexical Items Which Signal Text Relationships

These words are best learned within the context of texts which are "ideal types" of various organizational patterns in English. In Part III.F., sample exercises (including signal words) are shown for four pattern types: chronology, listing, comparison/contrast, and cause-effect.

Approaches to Teaching Vocabulary

Direct Instruction

Many teachers know the importance of pre-reading activities and recognize the fact that vocabulary should be learned in context. Before they assign a passage to the class, they often scan it and introduce some of the words which may be unfamiliar to their students.

But this approach may not be the most effective way to teach vocabulary! It sends students the message that meaning resides in words, and that they should worry about the meaning of every word if they wish to understand a text. Actually, we are hoping to engender just the opposite mind-set in our students: meaning is constructed by the reader, and we can skip over words which are unfamiliar.

This does not mean that one or two key words to a passage should not be taught prior to reading a text. However, teachers should be careful to select "key words in the target passages" of the text (Beck, Perfetti and McKeown 1982, cited in Tierney and Cunningham, 1984).

> Tierney and Cunningham (1984) conclude that:
> An extensive and long-term vocabulary strand accompanying a parallel schemata or background-knowledge-development strand is probably called for. Instead of pre-teaching vocabulary for single passages, teachers should probably be pre-teaching vocabulary and background knowledge concurrently for sets of passages to be read at some later time.

Some practitioners continue to maintain, however, that within a narrow context, such as a specific academic discipline, key words should be selected for direct instruction. This, in fact, is recommended by reading specialists in Israel, who have had many years of experience in teaching academic reading in English. In a program syllabus, they list 1,070 words which their university students should learn (Berkhoff and Greenbaum, 1983).

Vocabulary in Context

Teachers can introduce vocabulary-in-context in several ways. For example, students can acquire strategies for understanding new words in context by working on exercises such as this one, modeled after Van Daalen-Kapteijns (1981, cited in McNeil 1987):

Sample Exercise E.9.

Directions: Read the clues and try to guess what. xxxxxx is. Work with a partner.

Mystery Word: What is xxxxxx?

 a. He was used to having many xxxxxx in his room, so his new room seemed dark.

 b. He studied at the library, where there were more xxxxxx.

 c. The best part about xxxxxx is that you can open them in warm weather, to get a breeze.

 What is xxxxxx? _____

Note: Some teachers use "nonsense" words in their vocabulary-in-context exercises. This may be counter-productive with ESL/EFL students, since "real" words and "nonsense" words may appear the same to them in English! Xxxxxx's are recommended instead.

Gipe (1979) "reasons that a familiar context will activate a learner's 'old information' or schema and that the new meaning will then be assimilated. By relating the new word to an existing schema, the learner is more likely to retain the meaning of the new word." (Cited in McNeil 1987.)

Gipe's "interactive context" method is a little different from the one shown above. The following sample exercise is modeled after Gipe:

Sample Exercise E.10. Three Chances to Guess the Word Meaning from the Context

Directions: Read each sentence. Try to guess the meaning of the word. Work with a partner.

 a. She was aware that her boss was a *misogynist* soon after she started working for him.

 Guess: A *misogynist* is _____.

 b. It is difficult for a woman to work for a *misogynist* because she is never sure of the reasons for his criticism.

 Guess: A *misogynist* is _____.

 c. She knew that no woman would advance in his company, so she told the *misogynist* that she was resigning.

 Guess: A *misogynist* is _____.

 A *misogynist* is a person who dislikes women. Think of something a

misogynist might do in a family. _____

Gipe (1979) found that, for both good and poor readers, this interactive context method was superior to three other methods:

 a. Associative method — students memorize words paired with a short definition or a synonym.

   b. Category method — students are given categories in which they already know some words, learn new ones.

   c. Dictionary method — students look up words in dictionary, then write a sentence for each word.

Another way to develop word meanings in context is to engage students in concrete activities which require them to learn new terminology in print. For example, students can cook a meal together (recipes), plan a field trip (schedules and information brochures), or organize the class library (books and magazines).

These activities all require reading and learning new words. They are also low-anxiety activities during which students may feel more comfortable about taking risks in language learning.

Mahon (1986) recommends sentence completion exercises for building the context-using strategy. In fact, many students have enjoyed this type of exercise, which may be found in a kit called *Reading for Understanding* (Science Research Associates 1965). In this kit, cards with brief passages for sentence completion are organized at 100 increasingly difficult levels. This makes it a very useful set of materials for individualizing student practice. Similar exercises may be found in *Reading Power*.

Sample Exercise E.11.

Directions: In each passage, the last sentence is not finished. Choose the best ending. Check your work with a partner. Do you agree?

  1. Coffee grows in places with warm climates. In some parts of the world, the land is good for growing coffee. But the winters are too

    a. cold.   b. dry.   c. short.   d. cloudy.

  2. In Sweden, the summer days are very long. The sun shines for many hours. But the winter is very dark. The days are short because the sun sets

    a. very late   c. at midnight.
    b. are beautiful.   d. very early.

  3. In every country there is a different kind of money. For example, you may plan to go from Japan to the United States. Then you must change yen to

    a. cash.   b. dollars   c. money.   d. airplanes.

  4. In New England, the weather changes often. It may be sunny in the morning. Then it can be very cold and rainy in the afternoon. That is why a famous writer said: "If you don't like the weather in New England,

    a. go home."   c. bring an umbrella."
    b. wait a few hours."   d. listen to the radio."

  5. My favorite book is about the life of Charles Dickens. He was a famous English writer. It is a very interesting story. The best part is about

    a. airplanes.   c. his childhood.
    b. the economy.   d. the mountains.

(from *Reading Power*)

Vocabulary Development Through Extensive Reading

Researchers maintain that this is the most effective way to gain knowledge of new words.

- Krashen (1985:105)

    "Reading exposure will result in considerable language acquisition in the form of vocabulary growth and grammatical development."

- McNeil (1987:119)

    "Hence, a most effective way to produce large-scale vocabulary and to independently learn noninstructed words is to engage in a lot of reading."

See also Nagy, Herman and Anderson (1985).

ESL/EFL students are almost always concerned with their vocabulary development, but they often prefer to be assigned lists of new words to memorize. In order to assure them that they are acquiring vocabulary by extensive reading, they can be encouraged to start individual dictionaries based on their own reading. When they come across a word in their reading which they really want to remember, they can either make a card for it or list it in a notebook which has been paginated alphabetically. They should write down the word, the sentence they found it in, and their interpretation of its meaning in that context. They may also include the title of the book and the page number. They can use this list for personal vocabulary development.

For additional information on teaching vocabulary, see Long and Richards (1987), Section Ten.

F. TOPICS AND MAIN IDEAS

Although many reading specialists agree that a focus on specific comprehension skills is essential for ESL/EFL students (Eskey 1986, Grabe 1986, Johnston 1983, Nuttall 1983), there is no agreement about the order in which the remaining skills discussed in this part should be taught. Many have found that teaching overall patterns of text organization is useful for introducing work on topics and main ideas. But others, including this author, have found that it is more effective to begin by teaching the students to recognize topics. By beginning with simple topics, students can learn to approach the text in increasingly complex ways, and they can use their knowledge of topics later to help them in identifying overall textual patterns of organization.

It seems that every comprehension exercise and reading test includes this question:

"Choose the best main idea statement for this passage."

Finding the main idea is a complex task. It requires a finely tuned estimate of the parameters of the topic which the author had in mind as well as an interpretation of the author's intended expression about that topic.

Often, instruction in the skill of finding the main idea is based on repeated practice in answering the "main idea" question, presumably in the belief that students can learn this skill by trial and error. Actually, stating the author's main idea requires a series of thinking processes which students can learn. By learning how to break the main idea task into logical parts, students can become aware of the processes involved and can apply these steps in answering the "main idea" question.

By learning to identify topics, students will be able to see the connection between a text and previously formed schemata. This will help them notice how the details in the text relate to each other. And because English discourse is usually topic-centered, while the discourse in other languages may or may not be (Gee 1985:13), it is especially important that teachers give students the opportunity to develop this skill.

Furthermore, we know that some cultures do not define reading as we do in English, and so the whole notion of reading analytically or critically (reading to learn) is new to a good many ESL/EFL learners. Thus, it is essential that they learn how to think in terms of topics and generalizations in English texts if they wish to become proficient in the kind of reading required in English-speaking schools, universities, and businesses.

Some teachers may notice a similarity between some of the reading skills exercises and exercises they have used in teaching writing. This makes sense, since writing and reading are inseparable processes. In fact, working on reading skills such as these often results in improved writing and revising abilities.

Sequencing the Exercises

Since classifying and generalizing are thinking processes, exercises for practicing these skills are best presented in a developmental sequence, proceeding from simple to more complex cognitive tasks. As always, the students will learn faster and will be able to transfer their learning to other reading assignments if they are aware of the rationale behind the exercises (Brown, Armbruster, and Baker 1986). The sequence of exercise types listed here has been effective for teaching reading to native speakers of English as well as to ESL/EFL students:

1. Finding the topic of a list of words.

2. Stating the topic of a list of words.

3. Stating the topic of a list and telling which of the words in the list does not belong.

4. Sorting words into two lists and stating the topics of both lists.

5. Recognizing groups of sentences which make up a paragraph because of their relationship to a common idea.

6. Recognizing or stating the topic of a dialog or conversation.

7. Recognizing the topic of a paragraph.

8. Recognizing the topic sentence of a paragraph.

9. Inferring the author's main idea when it is not stated in the topic sentence.

10. Identifying the main idea of longer passages.

Notice that at each step, the complexity of the task is slightly increased, so that, for example, at level 1 the topic is given, but at level 2, the student has to think of a topic.

Materials for Teaching Topics Lessons

Two ESL/EFL textbooks which include this sequence for beginning or low intermediate students are: *Discovering American English: Reading* (Krantz, et.al. 1981) and *Reading Power* (Mikulecky and Jeffries 1986). Another source of exercises for such lessons is *Thirty Lessons in Outlining*, published at two levels:

Level I (Furbush, Ross, and Durrell 1975) and Advanced (Ross and Culliton 1971). Originally intended for native speakers of English, these two books are also effective for ESL/EFL students. Some of the sample exercises on the following pages include excerpts from *Reading Power* and from *Thirty Lessons in Outlining (Level I and Advanced)*.

After working through the exercises in this section, you will probably notice that while the format may be interesting and engaging, the content may not be ideal for your own classes. In fact, the exercises here, like others in this book, are best used as models. You can write your own exercises in very little time, and you can make sure that the content is suited to the interests and abilities of your own students. As usual, it is important to keep the language simple enough so that the main challenge comes from the thinking processes involved in the task.

When students work on exercises like these, it is essential that they do so in pairs, triads, or small groups. The work is fun that way, and the students learn from each other, using English as they work together. But most importantly, the students can practice new ways of talking about a text. This is how they can learn to think about language in an analytical way which may be very different from their usual approach to written language. In fact, they can develop literate skills which are the basis for school success in English.

Some teachers have found, however, that students from certain cultural groups resist working in pairs or groups. They say that they will not learn from another student and that they will work more efficiently on their own. This is a delicate situation. The interaction between students is fundamental to these lessons. Students' ability to explain their thinking to each other is equally important. If you explain the purpose of the collaborative work, most students will not continue to resist. As you work through the first few lessons below on topics of lists, the gradual development of skills will become obvious:

- Identify the general topic by sampling the list and noticing the possible ways that the items could be related to each other.

- Predict or look for a word which matches your inner notion of the general category that the words on the list might belong to.

- Ignore, temporarily, the words you do not recognize.

- Recognize that words you do not know are also members of the category you have named and now you have learned new examples of that category.

- Review and reinforce vocabulary and classifications you already know.

Those are some of the processes which the students need to talk about as they work together on similar topics exercises. The entire topics-to-main ideas sequence of lessons need not take a lot of time. Students usually catch on to the thinking process rapidly, and you should be careful to move on as soon as the class is ready to do so.

Learning to Recognize and State the Topic

Sample Rationale

Whenever you read, you try to connect what you are reading to what you already know. In order to make those connections quickly and accurately, it is important to know what you are reading about. For example, in the passage below, the topic is not given. Notice how difficult it is to make sense of it.

> The first time you try it, ask someone to help you. You may fall if no one holds you up. It is a good idea to start on the sidewalk. The street may be dangerous. After you start, do not stop. Try to go faster. That will help you to stay up. Remember, even little children can do this. And once you learn how, you will never forget!
>
> (Mikulecky and Jeffries 1986:21)

The exercises we will work on now will help you to get the habit of always asking yourself, "What is the topic?"

You should work with another student on these exercises, because then you will learn how to talk about your reading and your understanding of the text. The more you talk about your thinking, the better you will read.

The topic is: Riding a Bicycle.

Sample Exercise F.1. Recognizing the Topic

Directions: Read each list of words below. In each list there is a word that tells about all the other words. Find that word and write it on the answer sheet.

 1. pepper   nutmeg   cinnamon   spices   cloves   ginger
 2. beetle   fly   grasshopper   insects   bee   mosquito   butterfly
 3. wheat   grain   oats   rye   barley   corn
 4. Mercury   Venus   Earth   Planets   Jupiter   Saturn   Neptune
 5. locket   bracelet   necklace   ring   earring   jewelry
 6. flavours   lime   lemon   orange   chocolate   vanilla   peppermint
 7. dodgeball   jump rope   soccer   baseball   chess   football   bingo
     games   checkers
 8. arithmetic   spelling   subjects   reading   science   music
 9. ocean   sea   river   lake   water   pond   stream
     gulf   bay
10. mountain   valley   hill   plain   land   field
11. crayon   scissors   pen   pencil   ruler   eraser   supplies
12. fireman   workers   police   baker   teacher   plumber   doctor
13. doors   windows   exits   mouseholes   trap doors   fire escapes
14. loafers   slippers   rubbers   boots   footwear   oxfords
     bucks   sneakers
15. men   women   people   children   boys   students   girls

(from *Thirty Lessons in Outlining Level 1*)

Sample Exercise F.2.

Note: This is the same kind of lesson, using beginning level vocabulary which has already been learned by the class.

Directions: In each group of words and phrases, there is a word or phrase which tells about all the others. Find that word or phrase and circle it. The first one is done. Be sure to work with another student.

1. brush your teeth   wash the car   clean the garage
   fix the TV   things to do at home   wash the windows

2. basement   bedroom   bathroom   house   living room
   dining room   garage   attic

3. restaurant   bakery   bank   supermarket   library
   post office   places to go   hospital   bookstore

4. squirrel   dog   cat   animal   elephant   horse

5. lemonade   coffee   drink   tea   coca cola
   orange juice   seltzer   milk   ginger ale

6. Miss Johnson   Jim   Mary   People   Mrs. Olson
   Liz   Alan   Ernie   Judy

7. dancing   activities   studying   singing   playing
   drinking   eating   jogging

It is usually necessary to teach students the meanings of *general* and *specific*, terms which they will need to understand in order to work on the next exercises. A visual representation may help clarify their meanings:

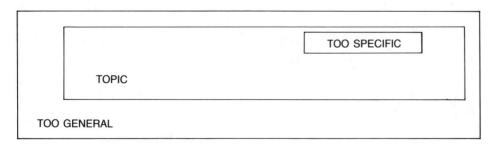

Sample Rationale

You will notice, as you work through the next exercises, that some of the topics that you think of are better than others.

Example: What is the best topic for this group of words?

> knife   fork   spoon   cup   plate   bowl
> glass   dish   chopsticks

> Topic: *kitchen equipment*

In the example above, the topic "kitchen equipment" is too general. A better topic would be "things people use for eating and drinking." A topic such as "dishes" would be too specific.

Sample Exercise F.3. General and Specific Terms

Directions: For each of these lists of words, find the topic below which describes it most exactly. Although more than one topic may fit a list, there is one topic which fits best because it is neither too general nor too specific. Work with a partner. The first one is done for you.

1. *American rivers*
   Mississippi
   Chicago
   Rio Grande
   Missouri
   Hudson

2. _____
   bus
   train
   motorcycle
   bicycle
   automobile

3. _____
   Kenya
   Tanzania
   Nigera
   Zambia
   Botswana

4. _____
   ice cream
   cake
   cookies
   pudding
   pie

5. _____
   lobster
   mussels
   oysters
   clams
   periwinkles

6. _____
   necktie
   shirt
   trousers
   jacket
   vest

Topics

Animals
Shell fish
Men's Clothing
Desserts
American rivers
African countries
Transportation

Sea animals
Clothing
Foods
Rivers
Countries
Zodiac signs
Land transportation

Sample Exercise F.4. Thinking of the Topic (High Beginning Level)

THINKING OF THE TOPIC

Write the topic. Work with another student. Try not to use the dictionary.

EXAMPLE

knife   fork   spoon   cup   plate   bowl
glass   dish   chopsticks

TOPIC: _kitchen equipment_ _____

---

1. Venezuela   Mexico   China   Canada   Germany

   TOPIC: _____

2. hospital   factory   library   school   hotel   bank

   TOPIC: _____

3. table of contents   index   title page   chapters   glossary
   cover   words   pages

   TOPIC: _____

4. French   Latin   Greek   Japanese   English
   Chinese   German   Arabic

   TOPIC: _____

5. physics   chemistry   astronomy   biology   geology

   TOPIC: _____

6. cheese   milk   ice cream   butter   cream   yogurt

   TOPIC: _____

(from *Reading Power*)

Sample Exercise F.5. Stating the Topic (Advanced Level)

Directions: Write a topic for each group of words. Make sure your topic is neither too general nor too specific. Work with another student.

1. merchant   director   general manager   sales manager
       buyer   accountant   chief executive officer

2. teller   auditor   loan officer   office manager
       president   accountant   mortgage officer

3. floppy   hard disk   menu   monitor   graphics card
       double-density disk   software   hardware

4. loam   fertilizer   rake   shovel   seeds   hose
       sprinkler   ground limestone   mulch

5. hosiery   lingerie   leather goods   shoes   men's clothes
       sportswear   housewares   linens

   Notice that for some of the items in the next exercise, there is more than one possible correct topic, depending upon your interpretation. See especially item #2.

Sample Exercise F.6. Finding the Topic and Omitting the Item
Which Doesn't Belong

Directions: In each list of words there is a term which does not belong. Omit this term. On the answer sheet write a topic for the remaining items and list the words under the topic.

1. sanctuary   lair   bridge   citadel   fortress   ghetto   shelter
2. pediatrician   internist   obstetrician   surgeon   psychologist
   general practitioner
3. lever   pulley   wheel and axle   inclined plane   wedges
   screw   wheelbarrow
4. delta   continental shelf   mesa   butte   bay   archipelago
   mountain   plateau
5. surrey   dugout   sub   frigate   corvette   destroyer
   cruiser   PT boat
6. lens   retina   cornea   iris   optic nerve   vitreous humor
   semicircular canals   aqueous humor
7. flask   beaker   bunsen burner   test tube   battery jar   mortar
8. French   Latin   German   Spanish   Italian   Portuguese   Polish
9. Newton   Archimedes   Michelangelo   Curie   Mendel   Einstein
10. saddle   harness   hunters   carriage   draft   boxer

(from *Thirty Lessons in Outlining, Advanced Level*)

Intensive Reading Lesson

At this point, you can begin to ask the students to be specific about their statement of the topic when they preview passages for intensive reading lessons.

Sample Exercise F.7. Sorting a list into two topics.

TWO TOPICS

Each list has words about two topics. Write the two topics. Then write the words under topics. Work with another student.

1. chair   table   book   bookcase   desk
   magazine   newspaper   bed   chest   letter

   TOPIC 1 _____   TOPIC 2 _____

   _____   _____

   _____   _____

   _____   _____

   _____   _____

2. noun   clouds   sun   stars   planet
   adjective   verb   moon   article   pronoun

   TOPIC 1 _____   TOPIC 2 _____

   _____   _____

   _____   _____

   _____   _____

   _____   _____

3. chest   arm   penicillin   leg
   aspirin   quinine   valium   shoulder
   tetracycline   hip   neck

   TOPIC 1 _____   TOPIC 2 _____

   _____   _____

   _____   _____

   _____   _____

   _____   _____

(from *Reading Power*)

Note: You can write exercises similar to those above for students at any level of language proficiency. The format is useful for reviewing and reinforcing vocabulary which has already been presented, introducing new vocabulary items, and reinforcing semantic associations in the schemata students are developing in English. It cannot be emphasized too strongly that the lessons you write for your classes are usually the most effective because you include vocabulary which is appropriate to the level, background, and interests of your students.

Topics of Conversations

Sample Exercise F.8. (Intermediate Level)

Note: When students work on exercises such as the following, they practice inferring the topic when it is not stated. There are several ways to present the exercises. You can read the conversations aloud for the students, or the students can read them silently and then aloud to a partner. The exercises should *never* be presented by having two students read the conversation aloud for the whole class. Under those conditions, the focus is on pronounciation, not comprehension.

Directions: Read each conversation silently. Then discuss it with another student. Decide together on the topic of the conversation and guess where it takes place.

Conversation 1: A. I just bought this last week and I would like to return it.

  B. What seems to be the problem?

  A. It does not work. I was late for school every day this week!

  B. Well, I can give you another one of the same type.

  A. Will this one work?

  B. Yes, of course. We are very sorry for the trouble the other one caused you.

Topic: _____

Location: _____

Conversation 2: A. Do you think he's here yet?

  B. I hope not. They said he'd arrive about an hour before the performance.

  A. I think you're right. I can hardly wait to see him.

  B. Have you ever seen him before?

  A. Only on TV.

  B. Do you have your pen ready?

  A. Oh, look, there he is!

Topic: _____

Location: _____

Conversation 3. A. Is this Mr. Mackay?

  B. Yes. May I help you?

  A. Yes, I'd like some more information about the ad in today's *Times*.

  B. Maybe I can answer your questions.

  A. I'd like to know the hours and the salary.

Topic: _____

Location: _____

Topics of Paragraphs

Before students are asked to identify the topics of paragraphs, it is a good idea to make sure they have a clear idea of what makes a paragraph in English. Exercises such as the one below from *Tactics in Reading* (Niles et al 1965) or others from Bander's book, *From Sentence to Paragraph* (1980) are effective for this.

Sample Exercise F.9.

Central Idea: WHAT MAKES A PARAGRAPH?

Read the following carefully:

> The state of Maine was pleased to have a delegation of French potato wholesalers come to inspect the state's huge potato farms. Remains of prehistoric bears, elephants, deer, and bison have been discovered there. Along the way, the pilot swung the helicopter from side to side and moved it backwards. He commented that the two-pack-a-day smoker obtains what might be a fatal amount of nicotine if taken in a single dose. Therefore, the men were not surprised to hear that Dick Nen bashed a home run on his second time at bat as a major leaguer and that the bride had chosen a full-length gown of white satin with controlled skirt and short-sleeved jacket.

This looks like a paragraph, but if you can make sense out of it, you are superhuman. When is a "paragraph" a paragraph? When it is a group of sentences all of which help develop a **central point or idea**.

Try this one:

> At the start of the test, she pulled into traffic without giving an arm signal. Turning left out of the right-hand lane from Main into Montrose Avenue, she drove to the corner of Salem. Here her foot nervously felt for the brake, but missed it, and she went through a traffic light on yellow. Startled to see a 25-mile speed zone sign, she stole a glance at the speedometer. It registered 35. Perhaps the inspector hadn't noticed. She pulled up at last, stepping on the brake too hard, and stopped with a jerk at Motor Vehicle Department headquarters. She leaned back in the seat and sighed. Finally the officer broke the silence. "You should have turned the wheel toward the curb. Better luck next time."

Why is this a paragraph?

PART A. Which of these groups of sentences, with only minor changes and additions, could be made into a paragraph? Circle the letters of these groups.

A

1. The women of the country carry water jars on their heads.
2. African elephants have large floppy ears.
3. Mrs. Johnson won the bridge prize Thursday.
4. The time for action is now.
5. Air flight is less dangerous than rail travel.

B

1. The Buffaloes were led by halfback Bob Anderson, who scored two touchdowns.
2. The Buffaloes walloped the Cardinals 31-0 at Memorial Stadium yesterday.
3. George Heston tallied on a 66-yard gallop to open the scoring.
4. He passed 30 yards to Ed Boyle for another TD.
5. A five-yard aerial play from Heston to Boyle turned out to be the final score in the game.

C

1. Most members of the Third Estate of France were peasants.
2. The nobles made up the Second Estate.
3. The First Estate consisted of churchmen.
4. Another part of the Third Estate was made up of servants, laborers, and skilled artisans.
5. A small part of the Third Estate was made up of the middle class — doctors, lawyers, merchants, and businessmen.

D

1. Laura knew her mother hated to tell her the truth.
2. The First Lady addressed the group and afterwards conversed with several of the guests.
3. The Silver Star Hotel is by far the most elegant I have ever seen.
4. Riding down the Salt River in an inflated inner tube was exhilarating but sometimes frightening.
5. Two engineering students were working on the road construction project.

PART B. In each group of sentences, cross out the one which could not be in a paragraph with the other four because it does not lead to a similar central idea.

1. For breakfast Jack had pancakes, orange juice, two eggs, bacon, a bowl of cereal with a banana, and a glass of milk.

2. Between bells in the morning he went to his locker and hastily ate two candy bars.

3. At noon he piled his plate with spaghetti, pizza, two hamburgers, and french fries.

4. In the afternoon he ate three ice cream bars.

5. John wore his checked shirt to school.

Part C. Re-read the groups of sentences which you think can be paragraphs. Write a rule for what makes a paragraph. Work with another student.

Rule: A group of sentences makes a paragraph when _____

_____

_____

(from *Tactics in Reading II*)

Recognizing the Topics of Paragraphs

Students should learn that sometimes a topic can be almost correct but not good enough because it is either too specific or too general.

Sample Rationale

When you read and you ask yourself, "What is the topic?", it is important to be as exact as possible. In the example below, all three of these ideas are found in the paragraph. But which one is the topic? Which one is too general? Too specific?

a. Italian food _____

b. spaghetti in Italy _____

c. surprises in Italian food _____

Example:

The food in Italy sometimes surprises American tourists in that land known for its fine cooking. The Americans expect to find pizza and spaghetti as the main courses in the restaurants. But pizza is rarely found, and spaghetti is served as a part of dinner, before the main course, which is fish, chicken, or meat. Tourists are further surprised when they find a great difference between the food in northern and southern Italy. But no matter how surprised they are, tourists agree that the food in Italy is fantastic.

Which one is the best topic? Why?

Notice that all three of the paragraphs in the next sample exercise are about the same general topic. After the students have identified the topic of each individual paragraph, they are asked to write a topic for the whole page. This is much more natural than having single paragraphs about unrelated topics on the same page.

Sample Exercise F.10. Choosing the Best Topic

CHOOSING THE BEST TOPIC

A. Make a check after the best topic. Write "too specific" or "too general" after the other topics. Work with another student.

1

It is easy to make a good cup of tea. Just follow these steps. First, boil some water. Next put some hot water in the tea pot to warm it. Pour the water out of the pot and put in some tea leaves. You will need one teaspoon of tea leaves for each cup of tea you want. Then pour the boiling water into the tea pot. Cover the pot and wait for a few minutes. Now the tea is ready to drink.

a. good tea   _____

b. how much tea to use   _____

c. how to make good tea   _____

2

The first people to grow coffee beans lived in the Middle East. The Persians, Arabs and Turks were drinking coffee many hundreds of years ago. Then, in the 1600s, Europeans learned about coffee. They quickly learned to like it. Soon there were coffee houses in many European cities. Europeans took coffee with them when they travelled to new countries. That is how people in other parts of the world learned about coffee. Now coffee is very popular in North and South America, in Africa and in parts of Asia.

a. the history of coffee   _____

b. European coffee houses   _____

c. popular drinks   _____

3

In the United States orange juice is one of the most popular cold drinks. Most of the oranges for juice grow in Florida. In many homes around the country, orange juice is always served at breakfast time. It is also a favorite snack at any time of the day. When there is bad weather in Florida the whole country knows about it. Bad weather in Florida means fewer oranges. And that means more expensive orange juice!

a. cold drinks in the United States   _____

b. bottle orange juice   _____

c. orange juice in the United States _____

B. Write the topic for all three paragraphs. _____

You can design similar exercises, using readers and class texts, newspapers, magazines, and textbooks from other courses.

(from *Reading Power*)

Sample Exercise F.11. Stating the Topic of a Paragraph

Note: This kind of exercise is more difficult, because the student has to think of the words which name the topic of the paragraph.

Directions: Part I. Write the topic for each paragraph. Be sure it is not too general or too specific. Work with another student. Then do Part II.

A Famous Guitarist

A. Before 1907, most people did not consider the guitar a concert instrument. Andres Segovia gave his first concert that year, when he was only 14 years old, and thus began a career which would change the history of music. From 1907 until his death in 1987, Segovia devoted his life to playing the guitar, writing classical guitar music, and teaching.

Topic: _____

B. Segovia explained to news reporters that he knew he was born with an amazing gift of music, and that he tried out several other instruments before he decided to become a guitarist. He abandoned the other instruments, he said, because there were no good players in his small Spanish village. He grew to love the guitar because it expressed his human qualities and his special musical gifts.

Topic: _____

C. Segovia travelled all over the world to perform, and people grew to love the sound of his music. Composers wrote special pieces for him, and Segovia himself transcribed music composed for other instruments. The beauty of his music also inspired others to take up the classical guitar, and he was a master teacher. Many of his classes became so popular that there were often audiences who paid admission to watch him teach.

Topic: _____

Part II. Write a topic for all three paragraphs. Work with another student.

_____

Sample Exercise F. 12. (Advanced Level)

Note: Exercises like this one will train students to take the entire paragraph into account in determining the topic and to make sure that the topic is neither too general nor too specific. (Modeled after Bander 1980.)

Directions: Part I. Each of the following paragraphs contains a sentence which does not belong in it. Cross out that sentence, and explain why it does not belong in the paragraph. Write the topic of the paragraph. Work with another student. Then do Part II.

An American Sport

Part I.

1. The Los Angeles Lakers are a championship basketball team. Their home court is the Forum, a modern stadium near Hollywood, California, and among their fans are some of the biggest names in the entertainment industry. Most basketball teams are based in large cities. Whenever the Lakers play at home games, they can be sure that stars like Jack Nicholson and Johnny Carson will be there to cheer for them. They have won four championships in the past eight years.

Topic: _____

2. The Boston Celtics are also a championship basketball team. They have won the National Basketball Association trophy sixteen times! Their home court is the Boston Garden, an old stadium not far from the waterfront. Although few famous movie stars attend their games, the Celtics enjoy the respect and support of all of the people in the Boston area. Boston fans also support major league baseball and football teams. On nights when the Celtics are playing a final or semi-final game at home, the theaters and clubs are half empty — all the fans are either at the game or are watching it on TV.

Topic: _____

3. Basketball, like other sports, is big business in the United States. The teams are owned by people who view them as at least partly a financial investment, and each owner tries to make his team as profitable as possible. The TV networks make great profits from the commercial ads during basketball games. They are a great influence in deciding when to schedule games — they want prime time audiences. Other programs during prime time include mystery shows and quiz programs. The players profit financially, too. Some of the players are paid as much as a million dollars a year.

Topic: _____

Part II. Write the topic of all three paragraphs.

_____

Intensive Reading Lesson

At this point, you can ask the students about topics of specific paragraphs within a passage.

Identifying the Topic Sentence

Sample Rationale

In some paragraphs, the topic is stated in one sentence. That is called the topic sentence. If you can find the topic sentence quickly, you can read the whole paragraph much faster and you can understand it better.

Example

We really are glad that we bought a VCR. We used to be so tired after work that we rarely had the energy to go out to the movies. Nowadays, we often stop off at the video shop on the way home from work and pick up one or two movies. We can stay at home, relax on a comfortable sofa or in bed, and snack from the near-by kitchen while we watch a movie. We can re-run parts of the movie, or put it on "pause" in order to stop and talk. Ah, that's the life. Thank you, VCR!

Topic: _____

Which sentence tells the reader what the topic is?

We really are glad we bought a VCR.

What do the other sentences do? They give some reasons why it is a good idea to have a VCR.

Sample Exercise F.13.

Directions: Each group of sentences makes a paragraph. Underline the sentence which tells about all of the other sentences in the group. Work with another student. Explain your answers.

Group 1
Television news can be very misleading.
Only bad news and sad stories are shown.
The news reporters do not tell all of the details.
Many important stories are not reported on the television news.

Group 2
Every day the television news reports on fires and accidents.
Many of the news stories are about illness and dying.
Only bad news and sad stories are shown.
Some of the news stories are about bad government.

Group 3
The television news reporter has only one or two minutes to report on each story.
Many news stories are not reported on television news programs.
The time is so short that the news editor leaves out some stories.
(Modeled after Moore, et. al. 1979)

Sample Exercise F.14. (Advanced Level)

Directions: Part I. Write the topic for each paragraph. Then underline the sentence with the topic stated in it. Remember to do Part II. Work with another student.

A Popular American Pastime

Part I.

1. People who are lucky enough to be within a day's drive of the wilderness areas of Maine have the opportunity to enjoy an exciting experience: white-water rafting. In the past, only wealthy people who could afford to fly out to the Grand Canyon could experience this adventure. But now people can go rafting on rivers which are not too far from several eastern cities, and several expedition companies offer complete guide service to rafters. It isn't necessary to own any of the equipment, not even a map.

Topic: _____

2. White water refers to a river which moves swiftly over rocky areas, up and down hills, and winding sharply through the forest. As the water rushes, it becomes filled with air bubbles and it actually looks white. In fact, as rafters are traveling along a river, they can spot dangerous areas ahead by looking for areas of white water. White water can be very dangerous, and rafters must be willing to risk being dunked in the river when their raft tumbles over waterfalls.

Topic: _____

3. Most rafting companies offer overnight rafting trips. In some cases, this may mean that several rafts of people will start out from the base camp with their food supplies, sleeping bags, tents, and other necessities packed onto the rafts. In other expeditions, the supplies, tents, and sleeping gear are trucked to the place where the rafters will spend the night. Often the guide is quite an accomplished chef, and the evening meal around the campfire is a gourmet event. Sleep comes easily to rafters, who have been out in the fresh air and sunshine all day.

Topic: _____

4. Almost anyone can go rafting. Very little heavy lifting or paddling in required. Some paddling, lifting of rafts, and hiking are all that is demanded. One year, a man took his 13-year-old daughter on a two-day rafting trip in Maine. He was afraid that it would be too tough for her. But she had no problems. In fact, she raved about her adventures for a year afterward, and convinced her mother to go along the next year.

Topic: _____

Part II.

What is the topic of the four paragraphs together?

_____

Write a topic sentence for all four paragraphs together.

_____

_____

_____

Sample Exercise F.15. (Intermediate Level)

This is an effective exercise because it demonstrates that all of the other sentences in a paragraph are details which support the topic sentence, and because it points out that topic sentences are most often, but not always, located at the beginning of a paragraph.

Finding the Topic Sentence

Often a writer makes it easy for you to grasp the central idea of a paragraph by stating it for you in a **topic sentence**. A topic sentence usually appears at the beginning of a paragraph, but may occur in other places as well. Notice how the topic sentence (in bold type) in the paragraph below focuses your attention on the central idea:

Of all the kinds of silver jewelry made by the Navajo Indians of Arizona, the bracelet is the best known. It is the piece most frequently bought by tourists as a souvenir. The wholesalers of Navajo-made silver, whose stores are mainly in Gallup, New Mexico, and Flagstaff, Arizona, sell more bracelets than all other types of silver combined. The Navajos themselves wear more bracelets than any other article of jewelry. Men as well as women wear them.

The topic sentences of the paragraphs that follow have been omitted and indicated by blank lines. Read each paragraph and think what the central idea should be. From the list of topic sentences at the bottom of the page, choose one that will best fit each paragraph. Write the letter of this sentence in the blank space in the paragraph. There is one sentence that you will not use.

1. _____. Much of this trade is with Pueblo Indians. The western Navajos carry on trade with the nearby Hopi villages. The central and southern Navajos trade dies and finished jewelry to the Zuñi, especially when they go to the Zuñi peublo in December for the festival of Shalako. Navajos living in the "four corners" area where Arizona meets New Mexico, Colorado, and Utah, also trade with the Utes, exchanging silver for Ute beadwork and buckskin.

2. _____. A silversmith does the Navajo a favor when he sells him jewelry for a high price, because then the buyer can boast about how much he paid. The first thing a Navajo says when complimenting another person on a piece of jewelry is, "That's pretty. How much did you pay for it?" A Navajo wears jewelry in order to display his wealth. He gets the same satisfaction from appearing at a squaw dance bedecked in silver and turquoise as he does when he gathers his sheep and goats together at the sheep dip where other Navajos come with their flocks.

3. Silver is also worn for its decorative effect. _____. If he has pawned all his jewelry at the trading post and is going somewhere, he borrows his relatives' jewelry; he would feel undressed and conspicuous if he were not wearing any. When a visitor to the reservation wanted to photograph an elderly Navajo, the Indian declined, saying "No, I don't have any of my turquoise and silver on. People who see the picture will say, 'Why, that Navajo doesn't have anything at all.' I would feel like a chicken with all its feathers plucked out."

4. Fifty or sixty years ago, massive, heavy pieces with bold, simple designs were considered beautiful. Twenty years later, jewelry had become more elaborate in form, and Navajo silversmiths were beginning to cover the surface of their bracelets and other pieces with curving designs applied with metal stamps or dies. More recently there has been a strong influence from the Zuñi Indians, and most Navajos today prefer silver set with rows or clusters of turquoise stones. _____.

a. Bracelets, rings, and necklaces have become an essential part of a Navajo's attire.

b. The Navajos trade their silver with other Indians of the Southwest.

c. In their jewelry, the Navajos use many designs that have a symbolic meaning.

d. It is evident that over the years there has been a change in the ideas of the Navajos as to what constitutes beauty in silver jewelry.

e. The Navajos think of their jewelry mainly in terms of dollars-and-cents values.

(from *Tactics in Reading I*)

Intensive Reading Lesson

You can include a discussion of the topic sentences in the passage. If there are some paragraphs without topic sentences, students can try to write one.

Stating the Main Idea

We have sort of sneaked up on the notion of main idea. Once students have had practice in thinking in terms of generalizations with supporting details, they need to learn that the main idea is a statement *about the topic*.

The notion of main idea is somewhat murky among reading specialists. Also referred to as the central idea, central focus, controlling idea, or main point, this concept is often confused with the topic sentence because quite often the topic sentence does state the main thought of a paragraph.

In this book the main idea is defined as the idea which the author wishes to express about the topic. Sometimes a topic sentence states the main idea and sometimes it does not.

Reading for main ideas makes it possible for the reader to recognize what is important and what can be skipped over in a text. The ability to grasp main ideas is also essential for skimming, summarizing, and paraphrasing. Students who learn to state the topic precisely and to recognize the supporting details and their relationship will be able to face "main idea" questions with confidence, because they have learned an analytical approach to answering them.

Sample Rationale

The topic tells you what the author is writing about. If you know the topic of a paragraph or passage, you know half of what you need to know. You also need to find out what the author thinks about the topic. Then you have the *main idea*.

When you know the main idea, you know what is important and what you can skip over. You can summarize a text and you know what to mark if you are studying a textbook.

These three paragraphs are about the same topic. Do they all tell the same *idea* about the topic?

a. Elephants are the largest land mammals in the world. They live on two continents, Africa and southern Asia. African elephants are larger and have great ears like fans. Asian elephants are called Indian elephants. Both kinds of elephants are majestic animals and very popular in zoos and circuses. They have been used for centuries as man's helpers in large building projects.

Elephants are_____

_____

b. Both the African and Indian elephants have strong, tough skin and long, lovely tusks. That is their problem. Elephants are in danger. People kill these animals in order to use their skin and their tusks. Because of the massive killings, elephants are dwindling in number and it is feared that by the end of the century, these huge mammals may be extinct.

Elephants are_____

_____

c. Elephants are a problem in some parts of Africa. In areas where the largest herds exist, they have become giant pests to the farmers. No fence is strong enough to keep these monsters away from the crops. Elephants go where they wish, destroying food crops and farm buildings, and wreaking havoc with the livestock. African farmers wonder if they can allow the elephants to continue to exist in their vicinity.

Elephants are_____

_____

The topic of all three paragraphs is the same: Elephants. But each paragraph expresses a very different idea about elephants. It is important to read for the topic AND for the idea the author expresses about that topic.

Sample Exercise F.16.

Read each paragraph. Ask yourself, "What is the topic? What is the main idea?" Write the topic beside the best main idea.

1

Clothes can tell a lot about a person. Some people like very colorful clothes. They want everyone to look at them. They want to be the center of things. Other people like to wear nice clothes. But their clothes are not colorful or fancy. They do not like people to look at them. There are also some people who wear the same thing all the time. They do not care if anyone looks at them. They do not care what anyone thinks about them.

a. _____ are colorful.

b. _____ can tell a lot about a person.

c. _____ always look nice on some people.

2

It is important to bring the right clothes when you travel. If you are going to a cold country, you should bring warm clothes. Be sure you have a hat and gloves, too. If you are going to a hot country, you need different clothes. You do not want heavy or dark clothes. In hot weather, light clothes are best. If you are going to a city, you may need some nice clothes. You may want to go to a special restaurant or a concert. It is different if you are traveling by bicycle in the country. Then you will want comfortable clothes. But one rule is the same for all travelers. Do not bring too many clothes!

a. _____ for warm weather are light.

b. _____ are important when you travel.

c. _____ can be heavy.

3

Clothes today are very different from the clothes of the 1800s. One difference is the way they look. For example, in the 1800s all women wore dresses. The dresses all had long skirts. But today women do not always wear dresses with long skirts. Sometimes they wear short skirts. Sometimes they wear pants. Another difference between 1800 and today is the cloth. In the 1800s, clothes were made only from natural kinds of cloth. They were made from cotton, wool, silk or linen. But today, there are many new kinds of man-made cloth. A lot of clothes are now made from nylon, rayon, or polyester.

a. _____ of the 1800s were beautiful.

b. _____ are made of man-made cloth.

c. _____ today are different from the clothes of the 1800s.

(from *Reading Power*)

Sample Exercise F.17.

Stating the Central Idea

After you have read the first paragraph below, ask yourself two questions: (1) What is the paragraph about? (2) What is the main understanding the author wants me to have about this subject?

Your answer to the first question will be the **topic** of the paragraph. Write this topic in the space provided. Then choose from the list that follows the paragraph the group of words that goes best with your topic to make a statement that answers the second question. Write X in front of this statement. The topic you have written plus the group of words you have selected will make a statement that is the **central idea** of the paragraph.

1. Small compact cars have become a familiar sight throughout the United States. A steadily increasing number of people favor these cars. They appreciate the low cost of operating a small car that goes 25 to 30 miles on a gallon of gas. In view of the many expenses involved in operating a car today, owners consider this an important saving. They also point out that the original purchase price of the compact car is considerably less than that of most of the bigger models. In addition, owners praise the increased maneuverability of their small cars. With parking space at a premium in most cities today, a small car that can easily move in and out of a tight space solves a problem for many drivers. People who select the compacts are likewise pleased with the simplicity of their styling. No wonder automobile companies are increasing their production of small compact models. _____

_____

_____ are more economical to operate.

_____ are popular for several reasons.

_____ have a small market.

_____ are suitable for every use.

2. A trip to Europe is a fascinating experience for many reasons, not the least of which is breakfast. At an English hotel this meal is a hearty one: juice, cereal, milk, bacon, eggs, toast, jam, and coffee. A short trip across the Channel and you are in Holland. The Dutch breakfast seems to be missing a few items. However, slices of cheese and ham, sweet dark bread, jam, butter, and coffee make an appetizing meal. In a Belgian hotel, breakfasts grow still smaller. Gone are the Dutch ham and cheese, but rolls, butter, jam, and coffee will satisfy most travelers. Breakfast changes again in a Parisian sidewalk café. While most Frenchmen content themselves with several cups of strong black coffee, the tourist often makes use of a basket of rolls and a plate of butter that are also offered. _____

_____ consist of many different kinds of food.

_____ are very unlike American breakfasts.

_____ are a surprise to the foreigner visiting Eruope for the first time.

_____ vary in size and in offering from country to country.

3. People came from miles around the small Pennsylvania town to see the first run of the steam locomotive, the *Stourbridge Lion*. The engineer refused to let anyone ride with him — perhaps because neither the engine nor the trestle had been tested. As the signal to start was given, there was a moment of suspense. Then, slowly, the wheels began to turn. Cheers went up as engineer Allen opened the throttle wide and began his historic trip. All along the route, men waved their hats, small boys shouted, and women stared in amazement as the *Lion* thundered past at the fantastic speed of ten miles an hour. Who would have believed that anything so big could move so fast without a horse to pull it! _____

_____ was an exciting event.

_____ occurred in Pennsylvania.

_____ took place in 1830.

_____ attracted many people.

4. As the first important traders who traveled by water, the Phoenicians constructed magnificent fleets of trading ships. Bold adventurers, they sailed their fragile boats bravely into the Atlantic. Wherever they went, Phoenicians spread the luxuries that made living more comfortable and pleasant, as well as the knowledge by which people could improve their way of life. As ship-builders, navigators, merchants, miners, metallurgists, gems engravers, and engineers, they were the first great pioneers. They even spread the use of the alphabet, opening unlimited horizons of learning. _____

_____

_____ **was carried on in ships.**

_____ **extended to every part of the world.**

_____ **benefited civilization.**

_____ **was the most important development of ancient times.**

(from *Tactics in Reading I*)

Sample Exercise F.18.

A. Read each paragraph. Ask yourself, "What is the topic? What is the writer's idea about the topic?" Then write the main idea sentence.

1

Population growth is a serious problem around the world. At the beginning of the 20th century there were about 1.5 billion people in the world. In 1984 the world population was 4.8 billion people. By the year 2000, it will be about 6.1 billion.

Main idea_____

2

This growth in population is not happening everywhere. For example, in Europe the population is not growing at all. Families in these countries are smaller now. Only about 2.1 children are born for every woman. The United States also has smaller families. Its population is only growing a little every year.

Main idea_____

3

But in other areas of the world, the population is growing very fast. This is true in parts of Africa, South America, and Asia. Countries in these areas have a difficult future ahead. Already, these countries have serious problems. First of all, food is a problem in many countries. Many people do not get enough to eat every day. There is not enough housing or work for everyone. Also, many people do not get education or medical care. A larger population will make all these problems worse.

Main idea_____

4

But there is some hope for change. It may be possible to slow down population growth. It happened in China, for example. In 1974, China's population was growing very fast. Then the people learned how to have smaller families. By 1984, the population was not growing fast anymore. This is an important change. China is the largest country in the world, with over one billion people. If China can make this change, maybe other countries can, too.

Main idea_____

B. 1. What is the topic of this page?_____

    2. What is the main idea?_____

_____

(from *Reading Power*)

Sample Exercise F.19. (Advanced Level) Writing the Main Idea When There Is No Topic Sentence

Directions: Part I. Read each paragraph. Decide on the topic. Then think about the idea that the author wishes to express about the topic. Write out the main idea in a complete sentence.

1. In every generation there are a few dreamers. Usually these people are driven by the contradictions and problems which confront them in society as it exists. They come to believe that an ideal society is possible, and they act on these beliefs by setting up experimental communities. Such communities, usually called utopian communities, have been proposed in many generations of American history. They never survive, but they serve as beacons for social change, reminding us that what exists is not permanent — society is built by humans and it can therefore be altered by them.

Topic: _____

Main Idea: _____

_____

2. In the mid-ninteenth century, utopian communities flourished in the United States. One of the most interesting was started by Bronson Alcott, the father of the author Louisa May Alcott. Called Fruitlands, this mini-society in Harvard, Massachusetts, was based on principles of self-sufficiency, cooperation and equality. Its name was derived from the dietary practices of the community: only food which grew above the ground was considered edible. Another utopian community of the same era was the famous Brook Farm, nearby in West Roxbury. Founded by a group of transcendentalists including the philosopher Ralph Waldo Emerson and the author Nathaniel Hawthorne, Brook Farm included philosophical discussions and musical events as part of their regular routine. Their strong belief in sexual equality was not shared by their neighbors. Both of these communities lasted for less than 25 years.

Topic: _____

Main Idea: _____

_____

3. Where are the utopian communities of the 1980's? It appears that the present generation of dreamers no longer seek to establish experimental communities on earth. It seems that only on a space platform or on another planet can people set up a planned social system. This is sad, because it reflects a loss of innocence and an attitude of hopelessness. Have our dreamers given up on planet earth?

Topic: _____

Main Idea: _____

_____

Part II. Topic of all three paragraphs _____

_____

Main Idea of all three paragraphs _____

_____

_____

_____

_____

Intensive Reading Lesson

The students can read seveal short (two- or three-paragraph) passages, and then state the main idea for each one. By now, you can include the following during an Intensive Lesson:

> Scanning (to select a passage)
> Previewing and Predicting (PreP)
> Determining the topic
> Reading to discover the main idea
> Guessing word meanings from context

G. PATTERNS OF TEXTUAL ORGANIZATION

Probably the most important reading comprehension skill that readers can develop is that of recognizing the organizational pattern of a text. Research has shown (Carrell 1984, 1985; Meyer 1977; Meyer and Rice 1987) that readers comprehend and remember best those materials which are organizationally clear to them, and that different organizational modes vary in accessibility to speakers of different languages (Carrell 1985).

ESL/EFL and other limited English proficient students require instruction in this important skill for several reasons. First of all, they may never have learned to notice patterns in texts, so they have not developed a schema for the concept of textual organization. Secondly, even if they have this schema, second language students are probably not aware of the ways that relationships between ideas are expressed in English prose. And they most likely do not know the vocabulary which signals text structure in English.

The exercises in this section demonstrate an approach to teaching several of the typical organizational patterns in English expository writing as well as the lexical items which signal those patterns. Textual clues to the pattern activate pre-formed expectations (concepts), which, in turn, encourage the reader to predict the content of the text. These predictions are then confirmed by further sampling of the text. Clearly, this enhances interactive processing of the text.

Students will learn to use such information as the topic, the main idea, and lexical signals as clues to the pattern of organization in a text. Building on previously-learned reading skills insures both continuity and systematicity in the reading course (Grabe 1986:44).

Introducing Patterns

Sample Rationale

Here are five figures. You will have one minute to study them. Then you will be asked to draw them from memory.

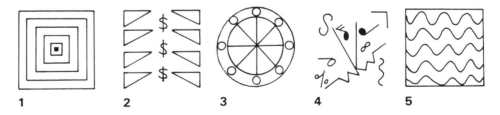

1   2   3   4   5

Which figure was the most difficult to remember? Why?

Of course, it is #4. That figure is not organized and there is no way to remember it as a pattern.

Patterns help us learn and remember in reading, too. Four of the simplest and most common are:

- *Generalization/Detail (Listing of related ideas)*

  Example: Judy really loves restaurants, and she would eat out every day if she could. One of her favorites is the Italian restaurant. Another is the deli and sandwich shop near her house. She also eats often at the Greek snack bar near the university.

- *Time Order (Chronology, Sequence, Process)*

  Example: Alan was checking his bicycle to make sure he could ride it to work safely. First, he checked the tires to make sure they had enough air. Then, he cleaned the frame and the rims of the tires. Next, he oiled the axle. After that, he checked the cable for the gears. And finally, he examined the brakes to make sure they were adjusted for quick stops in city traffic.

- *Comparison and Contrast*

  Example: Tomatoes are very popular in most parts of the United States, but most people prefer tomatoes grown in the home garden. There is a great difference between tomatoes from the supermarket and home garden tomatoes. The supermarket tomatoes have very little taste, their color is pale yellow-red, and they are almost as hard as rocks. On the other hand, home garden tomatoes are deep red, juicy, tasty, and tender.

- *Cause-Effect*

  Example: Boston has a very beautiful water front and harbor, but it is the dirtiest in the United States. The pollution is due to the old practice of draining all the waste water from the city into the harbor. Factories and hospitals dump many chemicals down the drains to the harbor. Ships in the harbor add to the problem by flushing out tanks there.

You will work on exercises to develop the skill of recognizing patterns of organization in reading. You will find that you can read better and remember more when you can identify the pattern in the text.

Note: For patterns exercises, it is important to choose passages which are linguistically and conceptually simple. At first, especially, the signal words should be very obvious. The main challenge should be recognizing the relationship pattern and the signal words.

Generalization/Details (Listing)

Sample Rationale

Often an author lists a few facts about a topic, perhaps to explain a main idea, support an opinion, or give some evidence about a general statement. In English, this is a very common pattern. It is sometimes called the listing pattern. Writers often use special signal words to let the reader know how the text is organized. Once you find the signal words and the pattern, it is easier to understand and remember the author's ideas.

Sample Exercise G.1. Lists in Sentences

Directions: Circle the numbers of the sentences which contain lists.

1. The three sisters enjoyed their trip to the zoo.
2. They saw many dangerous animals, including tigers, lions, and poisonous snakes.
3. They visited the bird exhibit, the children's zoo, and their favorite, the elephant house.
4. The girls were very hungry after walking around the zoo all morning.
5. They enjoyed hot dogs, root beer, and ice cream at the snack bar for lunch.

Sample Exercise G.2. Using Signal Words for Listing in Paragraphs

Example:

In this paragraph, the author wants to tell several facts or ideas about this topic: What makes a great vacation.

People have <u>many different ideas</u> about what makes a great vacation. <u>Some</u> people like to go away to the remote, silent forest, where they won't see anyone for days at a time. <u>Others</u> prefer to spend their days in an exciting city like New York, where they walk through crowded museums all day and dance at discos all night. <u>Still others</u> enjoy the seashore, where they can spend their days in the brisk salt air and allow the ocean waves to wash away their thoughts of home and work. <u>A few</u> people decide to be practical and spend their vacation time at home, doing major household projects, such as painting the house or re-building a porch.

The underlined words are signals to let the reader know that this paragraph lists some details to support a general idea.

Topic: vacations
Pattern Signal: many different ideas

Signals words	Details
some	like the forest
others	prefer the city
still others	enjoy the seashore
a few	use the time for practical jobs

Directions: In the next two paragraphs, the signal words are underlined. Write the topic, the signal words, and the details in the space below. Work with another student.

1. Jim's boss sent him a memo today about his work on his new job. In the memo, Jim's boss gave him <u>many reasons</u> to feel good about his work. <u>First</u>, the boss said that Jim had learned the technical parts of his new job very quickly. She <u>also</u> stated that Jim was getting along very well with all of the people in the office. <u>In addition</u>, she wrote that he was very kind and polite to customers on the phone, and that is very good for the business. <u>Finally</u>, she hinted that in a few days Jim would find a nice bonus in his paycheck.

Topic: _____

Pattern Signal: _____

Signal Words   Details

2. Although she enjoys her work, Mary often thinks of quitting her job, mainly because her boss has so <u>many unpleasant characteristics</u>. <u>First</u>, the supervisor never praises Mary when she has done an especially good job on one of her projects. <u>Second</u>, the boss does not know how to let her work on her own. He interferes and later he tells her that she does not know how to work alone. <u>Last</u>, he arrives late for work every morning, and he often takes long lunch hours.

Topic: _____

Pattern Signal: _____

    Signal Words   Details

Sample Exercise G.3. Recognizing and Using Signal Words for the Listing Pattern (Advanced Level)

Directions: In these paragraphs, the signal words are not underlined. You will find some of these signal words:

variety	for example	few	others	besides
also	another	some	main	second
numerous	in addition	first	many	several
furthermore	last			

Write the topic, the signal words, and the details for each paragraph. Work with another student.

1. Communicating by electronic mail (computer networks) has caused numerous changes in the way people relate to each other. First, the new "e-mail" services are rescuing the introvert from the telephone-equipped extrovert, because people who are too shy to call someone on the phone can send a message by computer. Second, e-mail allows a more democratic flow of information by introducing a new way of communicating which does not contain certain social cues found in other forms of communication (such as types of stationery or formal conversations between boss and employee). Also, the electronic message is instant, so there is no way to use pauses or delays to give hints about the underlying message, as often happens when people speak on the phone. Last, the messages are uniform and give no external clues to the sender's age, gender, race, or physical condition.

Topic: _____

Pattern Signal: _____

    Signal Words   Details

2. One advertising executive has stated that he does not use electronic mail for a variety of reasons. The main reason is that he has not yet mastered the system. But, in addition, he feels that it is a very impersonal way to communicate. He also thinks that e-mail is fast, slick and easy rather than thoughtful. Furthermore, he feels that you lose a lot of information when you use computer mail instead of talking to someone in person, especially the tone of voice and expression.

Topic: _____

Pattern Signal: _____

    Signal Words   Details

Note: The next exercise is a writing exercise. It is included here because one of the best ways to learn the importance of patterns is see them from the writer's point of view.

Sample Exercise G.4. Using Signal Words in Writing

Directions: Write a paragraph in a listing pattern. Start by writing a general statement about the topic. Then list several facts or details to support the statement. Use some of the signal words from the list on page 114. Write about one of these topics, or think of one of your own:

1. Why do people learn a second language?

2. What kinds of reading materials can you find in the library?

3. What are the biggest problems in the world?

Intensive Reading Lesson

Find several passages which are clearly written in the listing pattern with clear signal words. Instruct the students to preview the passages and then choose the one the whole class will work on together intensively.

    Students should be able to tell the topic and the main idea, and they should also be able to identify the listing signal words and tell the details which have been signaled.

Time Order (Chronological Order)

Sample Rationale.

In a passage with a Time Order pattern, the writer tells about some events in the order in which they happened.

TIME ORDER

Example A

Albert Einstein was born in *1879* in Ulm, Germany. He graduated from the
University of Zurich in Switzerland in *1905*. In *1905* he also did some of his most
famous work in physics. In *1919* he won the Nobel Prize for Physics. *Between 1919
and 1933* he lived in Germany and traveled a lot to talk to other scientists. Then
in *1933* he had to leave Germany because of Hitler and the Nazi party. He moved
to the United States. From *1933 until his death* he lived in Princeton, New Jersey.
He died on *April 18, 1955.*

What is the topic of this paragraph?_____

How can you tell this is a time order pattern?_____

You can tell because the signals in this paragraph are all dates. Each date
points to an event in the life of Albert Einstein. Here are all the signals. Write
the events:

Signals   Events

1879   _____

1905   _____

1905   _____

1919   _____

1919–1929   _____

1933   _____

1933–1955   _____

April 19, 1955 _____

Example B

This paragraph is about the same events as Example A. But the signal words
are different.

   Albert Einstein was born near the end of the 1800s, in Ulm, Germany. He
graduated from the University of Zurich in Switzerland at age 26. That was also
when he did his famous work in physics. Fourteen years later he won the Nobel
Prize for Physics. For the next ten years he lived in Germany. He also traveled
a lot to talk with other scientists. Then in the early 1930s he had to leave Germany because of Hitler and the Nazi Party. He moved to the United States.
From that time until his death he lived in Princeton, New Jersey. He died at the
age of 74.

Here are the signals. Write the events:

Signals   Events

near the end of the 19th century _____

at the age of 26   _____

That was also when   _____

Fourteen years later   _____

For the next ten years   _____

In the early 1930s   _____

From that time until his death _____

at the age of 74   _____

Dates are often signals for the time order pattern. Here are some other time order signal words:

first	next	soon	after	at last	finally	dates
last	later	before	while	then	times	

Sample Exercise G.5. Using Time Signals

Read each passage. Write the topic and underline the signals. Then write the signals and the events on the lines.

1

The Vietnam War began soon after World War II. At first, in 1946, the war was between the Vietnamese and the French. The government was French, but many Vietnamese people did not want a French government. They wanted the French to leave so they could have their own government. The Vietnamese fought hard, and slowly they won more and more land. By 1953, the French army was in trouble. They were not winning the war. French soldiers were dying and the war was costing a lot of money. So, in 1954, the French army stopped fighting and left Vietnam. That was the end of the first part of the Vietnam War.

Topic: _____

Signal	Events
_____	_____
_____	_____
_____	_____

2

The Second part of the Vietnam War began in 1954. After the French army left, there were two Vietnams: North Vietnam and South Vietnam. There were also two governments. But both governments wanted to be the only government for all of Vietnam. So from 1954 until 1960, the North and the South were fighting all the time. The North Veitnamese grew slowly stronger. By the beginning of 1965, the North Vietnamese were winning the war. But the United States government did not want the North Vietnamese to win. So in March 1965, the United States began to help South Vietnam. They sent guns and airplanes to help the South. At first, the United States sent only a few soldiers. But by July 1965, there were about 75,000 American soldiers in Vietnam.

Topic: _____

Signals	Events
_____	_____
_____	_____
_____	_____
_____	_____

(from Reading Power)

Sample Exercise G.6. (Advanced Level)

Directions: These paragraphs are in time order. Underline the signal words, and then write the topic and the signal words below. For each signal, write the event it points to. Show your work to another student. Do you agree? The signal words are already underlined in paragraph 1.

These signal words are often used to show time order:

first	soon	later on	at the end
next	later	in the meantime	at last
last	afterwards	in the beginning	not long after
finally	right away	eventually	immediately
during	after		
dates and times			

1. <u>By 1984</u>, NASA, the United States space program, had carried out many successful flights of the space shuttle. In fact, Americans were beginning to take the whole NASA program for granted. <u>Then</u>, the President announced that the next shuttle would carry a school teacher into space. <u>Immediately</u>, hundreds of school teachers from all parts of the country applied for the honor of being the first teacher in space. <u>During the next year</u>, these adventurous educators were tested and examined and trained, and <u>at last</u> the choice was announced: a teacher from New Hampshire, Christa MacAuliffe, would be the first teacher-astronaut.

Topic: _____

Signal words: Events:

2. Many months of preparation and training followed. First, Christa and all of the other astronauts went through intensive physical training, so that they would be in top condition for the flight. Then they all learned how to operate the delicate instruments on the space shuttle. Later, Christa planned special lessons which she would teach from space. Finally, they had learned all that they needed to know to be able to work together as a team in space. They were ready for the flight of the Challenger at last.

Topic: _____

Signal Words: Events:

3. Everyone knows what happened on that terrible day in January, 1986. Early in the morning, the Challenger crew had a good breakfast and discussed their plans for the work they would do during the flight. Later, they boarded a special van which carried them to the shuttle. The weather was a bit too cold, and some officials wondered if the blast-off should be postponed. After some discussion, they decided to go ahead. Then the Challenger took off, and it exploded immediately afterwards. There were no survivors.

Topic: _____

Signal Words   Events

Sample Exercise G.7. Time Signals in a Longer Passage (High Beginner Level)

Directions: In a longer passage, time order signals are even more helpful. Read this passage and underline the time signals. Write the topic and the signal words below.

Ballooning

The first kind of air transportation was not a plane. It was a balloon. People traveled by balloon one hundred years before there were planes or jet aircraft. Those early days of ballooning were exciting, but they were also dangerous. Sometimes the balloons fell suddenly. Sometimes they burned. However, the danger did not stop the balloonists.

The first real balloon flight was in France in 1783. Two Frenchmen, the Montgolfier brothers, made a balloon. They filled a very large paper bag with hot air. Hot air is lighter than cold air, so it goes up. The Montgolfiers' hot air balloon went up 1,000 feet in the sky.

Later that same year, two other Frenchmen ascended in a basket under a balloon. They built a fire under the balloon to make the air hot. This made the balloon stay up in the air for a few hours. But their balloon was tied to the ground. So it could not go anywhere.

The first free balloon flight was in December, 1783. The balloon flew for 25 minutes over Paris. It traveled about five and a half miles.

Very soon balloonists tried longer flights. A major event in the history of ballooning was the first long flight over water. In 1785, an American and a Frenchman flew over the English Channel. They left England on a cold, clear January day. After about an hour, their balloon began to descend towards the water. They threw out some equipment and food to make the balloon lighter. The balloon continued to fall, so they threw out almost everything in the basket — even some of their clothes. Finally, after about three hours, they landed in France, cold but safe.

During the 19th century, ballooning became a popular sport. There were balloon races in Europe. Balloons were also used by scientists to study the air and by armies in war time. After the airplane was invented, people lost interest in balloons. Planes were much faster and easier to control. But some people today still like to go up in balloons. High up in the balloon basket, they find quiet. They have a wonderful view of the world below.

Topic: _____

Signal Words: Events:

(adapted from *Reading Power*)

Sample Exercise G.8. Steps in a Process (Beginning Level)

Note: A sequence of steps is similar to time order.

Directions: Read this paragraph. Write the topic and the signal words below. Then write a step in the sequence of steps for each signal word. Work with a partner.

1. When you decide to take a trip, the planning can be fun. First, you have to decide where to go. Next, you need to look at maps and books about the place, and figure out how to use your time while you are there. Soon after that, you should talk to a travel agent to find out how you will travel, and how much it will cost. Then, if you are going to a country with a language different from yours, you may decide to learn a few phrases in that language. Finally, you need to make a packing list, and check to be sure that you have everything you need. After all of this, you can relax and have a great trip.

Topic: _____
Signal Words: Steps:

Sample Exercise G.9. The Steps in a Long Process

Note: As the students work together in sorting out the list of steps in this sample exercise, they will use the time order signal words orally quite naturally. When the class discusses the ordering of this sequence of steps, be sure to point this out to the students.

Directions: Read the passage and try to remember the order of the steps in making a submarine sandwich.

Hot Subs for Lunch

The name may be different in other parts of the world, but in Boston they are known as "subs" or submarine sandwiches. One of the most popular lunch items in town, a sub for lunch is typical for people from all walks of life, from the governor on down.

The best way to find out about subs is to go to a sub shop, where these wonderful sandwiches are the specialty. You will find huge ovens right behind the counter, because a real sub is served hot.

The sub sandwich maker usually says, "What kind of sub do you want?" The customer might answer, "Large Italian."

The man begins by taking a large, long bread roll from a plastic bag under the counter. He slices it lengthwise and puts in layers of Genoa salami, mortadella, and other cold meats, and tops that with provolone cheese.

Leaving the sandwich open, the sandwich chef places it on a metal tray and slides it into the oven. He bakes it until the meat is warm, the roll is toasty, and the cheese has begun to melt. Then he takes it out and calls out, "Whaddya want on yer large Italian?"

"Everything," is the reply. "Everything" means that he adds mayonnaise, salt, pepper, oil, and a sprinkling of oregano. But that is not all. He also puts in lots of chopped pickles, sliced onions, pickled hot peppers, sliced tomatoes, and crunchy chopped iceberg lettuce.

Finally, taking the sandwich in his hand, the sandwich maker folds the two sides together, carefully slices it in half, and wraps it in waxed paper. "For here or to go?," he asks. No matter which way you take it, you can be sure that you will enjoy lunch that day!

How did he make the submarine sandwich?

Below are the steps involved in making a submarine sandwich, but they are out of order. Write the numbers of the steps in the correct order. Try not to look back at the passage. Work with a group of three or four students.

 1. He carefully slices it in half.
 2. He adds liberal portions of chopped pickles.
 3. He places it on a metal tray.
 4. He wraps it in waxed paper.
 5. He takes a large bread roll out of a plastic bag.
 6. He folds the two sides together.
 7. He slices the roll in half lengthwise.
 8. He asks, "For here or to go?"
 9. He calls out "Whaddya want on yer large Italian?"
10. He allows it to bake until the meat is warm.

The steps should be:

(Modeled after Niles, et.al 1965)

Intensive Reading Lesson

Assign several different kinds of time-order and process passages. Students should be able to apply these skills:

Preview and Predict
Scan for specific information
State the topic
State the main idea
Recognize the pattern and tell the steps in order

Comparison-Contrast

Sample Rationale

A. Writers sometimes want to *compare* two things. In other words they want to explain how the two things are alike and how they are different. Then they use a *comparison* pattern.
For example:

Comparison of a Mercedes-Benz and a Volkswagen

1. How are they alike?
   a. Both have gasoline or diesel engines
   b. Both have four wheels
   c. Both are used for personal transportation

   d. Both are _____

2. How are they different?
   a. Purchase price
   b. Cost of fuel and maintenance
   c. Status
   d. Comfort

   e. _____

B. Sometimes a writer wants to explain only how two things are *different*. This is called a *contrast*.
For example: Contrast your country and the United States. How are they different?
a.

b.

c.

You can recognize the comparison/contrast pattern by noticing that the author is writing about *two things* and by noticing the signal words. When you know how to recognize this pattern, you will be able to understand and remember more when you read.

Sample Exercise G.10. Introductory Exercise

Directions: Preview this passage. Is it a comparison or a contrast? _____

How can you tell? _____
Read the passage. Then fill in the table below. Work with a partner. (The signal words are underlined.)

New York and San Francisco

There is quite a difference of opinion about the qualities of New York and San Francisco. Some people who have visited both cities say that there are some similarities. Both cities are exciting cultural centers, with many residents who come from countries all around the world. And the cities are alike in that they have lovely architecture and grand bridges. And, of course, both are port cities. On the other hand, people argue that the similarities end there, and the differences are important. New Yorkers are always in a hurry and are much less friendly than the people of San Francisco. And the streets in the California city are very clean and in good repair, unlike the mess one finds all over New York. There is much less crime in San Francisco than in New York. People in New York are always afraid when they are out on the street. The debate is fierce and may never be resolved.

Main Idea _____

_____

Signals of comparison/contrast pattern: similarities on the other hand

Signals of likeness:

Signals of difference:

How are New York and San Francisco alike?

_____

_____

_____

How are they different?

_____

_____

_____

Other signal words for the comparison/contrast pattern:
likenesses: like, as in, in the same way, similarly, both, also
differences: however, but, rather, yet, conversely, instead, different from, in
     contrast to, although, bigger than, on the other hand

Sample Exercise G.11. Using Comparison/Contrast Signals

Underline the signal words in each paragraph. Write the likenesses and differences on the lines.

1

In some ways English breakfasts are very similar to American breakfasts. In both countries people usually eat large breakfasts. English and American breakfasts both include several dishes. They may include some fruit juice, cereal, and then eggs and toast. In both places, there may also be some meat with the breakfast. However, there are also some differences between American and English breakfasts. In England, people usually drink tea in the morning. However, most Americans prefer coffee. The English usually do not eat sweet things for breakfast, but many Americans like sweet bread or coffee cake.

What is this paragraph comparing?_____

Likenesses   *Differences*

_____   _____

_____   _____

_____   _____

_____   _____

2

American breakfasts are very different from breakfasts in Italy. In general, American breakfasts are much larger than Italian breakfasts. Americans may eat several different foods for breakfast. They may eat cereal and eggs and toast. But Italians usually just have bread and coffee. Many Americans also like to eat some kind of meat. Italians almost never eat meat early in the morning. Finally, American coffee is different from Italian coffee. Americans do not drink strong coffee in the morning. Italians always like their coffee strong and dark.

What is the paragraph contrasting? _____

Differences

_____

_____

_____

_____

_____

(from *Reading Power*)

Sample Exercise G.12. Comparison (Intermediate Level)

**Part 1
Presentation**

Study the following table and identify:
a the characteristics which the eye and the camera have in common.
b the characteristics which make them different.

Characteristics	Eye	Camera
Needs light rays to function	✓	✓
Has a lens	✓	✓
Has a sensitive surface	✓	✓
Lens moves backwards and forwards	✗	✓
Curvature of the lens changes	✓	✗
A device regulates the amount of light that enters	✓	✓

Table 1 ✓ = yes   ✗ = no

Next, read these statements which compare the eye and the camera and complete Table 2 with ✓ or ✗ as in Table 1.

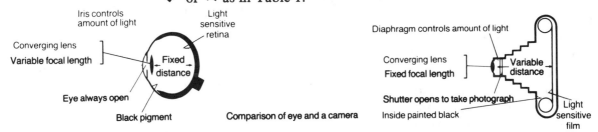

Comparison of eye and a camera

The camera and the eye are similar in many respects. They both need light rays in order to function. Both have a sensitive surface on which the image is formed. In the eye the image is formed on the retina. In the camera the image is formed on the film. As in a camera, the image on the retina is inverted.

Both the eye and the camera have a lens. The lens focuses the image on the sensitive surface. In the camera, the lens moves backwards and forwards. In the eye the curvature of the lens is changed. In this respect the eye differs from the camera.

Both the camera and the eye have a device to regulate the amount of light that passes through the lens. In the camera there is a shutter of variable speed and a diaphragm of variable aperture. In the eye the iris automatically adjusts the size of the pupil according to the intensity of light.

Both the eye and the camera are sensitive to light, shade and colour. The film records light, shade and colour. The eye perceives them but does not record them. The two eyes together produce a three-dimensional image. The camera lens produces a two-dimensional image.

The eye is more flexible than the camera. It can adapt more quickly to a wider range of light conditions. Both the camera and the eye can register small objects and distant objects. The camera performs these functions better than the eye.

Characteristics	Eye	Camera
The image is inverted		
The lens focuses the image		
Sensitive to light, shade and colour		
Records light, shade and colour		
Produces three-dimensional image		

Now answer the following questions:
a What is the eye's sensitive surface called?
b What devices in the eye and the camera regulate the amount of light that enters?
c What advantages do the eyes have over the camera?
d What advantages does the camera have over the eye?

(from *Reading and Thinking in English*)

Intensive Reading Lesson

Now that students have learned to use three patterns, you can assign one passage of each type. The students should preview the three passages and then predict the over-all pattern of each one. The class, as usual, should decide as a group which of the passages to read and discuss intensively. And, once again, you can ask them to apply all of the skills they have learned so far.

Cause–Effect Pattern

This is a difficult pattern for several reasons. First, unlike other patterns, the signals are often verbs. (The strong coffee *caused* me to stay awake all night.) As integral parts of sentences, they don't stand out the way the signal words for other patterns usually do. Furthermore, verbs forms can express the cause-effect relationship actively (The rain *caused* the flood.) or passively (The flood *was caused* by the rain.).

Second, cause-effect relationships are as likely to be single (What caused the flat tire?) as multiple (What were the causes of World War I? What were the effects of the flood?).

There is also the problem of word order. If students mistakenly assume that the thing named first is always the cause and the thing named second is the effect, they are in trouble! It is important to keep these factors in mind when selecting or writing items for teaching cause and effect relationship patterns, and it is best to begin with single cause-effect relationships which clearly show the connection between the passing of time and cause and effect (Zupnik 1988).

Sample Rationale

Causes and effects are part of our daily lives. It is important to learn how to recognize the cause-effect pattern when you read. But it not as easy as the other patterns.

> *Example:* I missed the bus this morning.
> I was late for work.

What happened first?   What happened next?
I missed the bus. ⎯⎯⎯⎯⎯⎯⎯→ I was late for work.
   (Cause)   (TIME)   (Effect)

When you read a passage with a cause-effect pattern, THINK:
"What happened first?"
Then you will know the cause.
A cause-effect sentence does not always put the cause first.

Because I missed the bus, I was late for work.
(Cause) ⎯⎯⎯⎯⎯⎯→ (Effect)

I was late for work *because* I missed the bus.
   (Effect) ◄⎯⎯⎯⎯⎯ (Cause)

In both sentences, *because* is the signal word. It is in the part of the sentence that tells the cause.

(Adapted from Zupnik 1988)

Sample Exercise G.13. Identifying Causes and Effects (Intermediate Level)

Directions: Part I. Study the following pairs of words and phrases. Which causes which?

THINK: Which one comes first? Then draw an arrow from the cause to the effect. The first one is done. Work with another student.

1. viruses ⎯⎯⎯⎯⎯⎯→ infectious diseases
2. epidemics   bacteria
3. headaches   colds and flu
4. improperly stored food   food poisoning
5. slow development   improper nutrition
6. swimming in pools   ear infection
7. heart trouble   diet high in fat
8. skin cancer   too much exposure to the sun
9. black lung disease   working in a coal mine
10. skiing   broken leg

Part II. For each pair, write a sentence. Begin each sentence with the statement on the left.

- If the arrow goes from left to right ⎯⎯⎯⎯⎯→ , use these cause/effect signal words:

cause	lead to	is the cause of	results in
can cause	gives rise to	brings about	produces

- If the arrow goes from right to left ←⎯⎯⎯⎯⎯ , use these cause/effect signal words:

is due to	is the result of	is caused by
results from	is produced by	is a consequence of
can result from		

Examples:

1. Viruses can cause infectious diseases.
2. Epidemics are produced by bacteria.

(Modeled after Moore, et.al 1979)

Sample Exercise G.14. (Intermediate Level)

Directions: Read each sentence. Underline and label the cause and the effect. Draw an arrow from the cause to the effect. Work with another student.

Example: Hepatitis can result in chronic ill health.
             C ←⎯⎯⎯⎯⎯⎯→ E

1. Coal-burning factories cause acid rain.
2. Stricter anti-pollution laws can lead to higher prices for consumers.
3. Acid rain can bring about the death of lakes and streams.
4. Forests have become diseased due to acid rain.
5. Coal burning also results in higher levels of sulfur dioxide in the air.
6. Sulfur dioxide pollution can result in higher infant death rates.
7. Coal burning causes the exterior walls of buildings to decay.
8. Strict anti-pollution controls may cause coal miners to lose their jobs.

Sample Rationale

Often there is not just a single cause and a single effect.

A. Sometimes one cause has many effects.

Fifteen inches of rain fell in Miami in four hours. As a result, all public transportation stopped, Kim's car would not start, Bob had to stay at home, and no one came to Al's party.

Cause: Fifteen inches of rain fell in Miami in four hours

Effects: All public transportation stopped
Kim's car would not start
Bob had to stay at home
No one came to Al's party

B. Sometimes one effect has many causes.

The car would not start this morning, the bus was 30 minutes late, I lost my office keys, and my secretary called in sick. Because of all of these problems, I had a terrible headache by lunch time.

Causes: The car would not start
The bus was 30 minutes late
I lost my keys
My secretary called in sick

Effect: Terrible headache

Sample Exercise G.15. (Beginning Level)

PART A On the left are two possible causes for the list of effects on the right. Write the letter of the effect under the most probable cause. Work with another student. Explain your choices to the class. Some of the effects can be used twice.

Causes:

Learning a new language

_____

Living in a new city

_____

Possible Effects:

a. Many headaches

b. Meet interesting people

c. Danger

d. Spending a lot of money

e. Going to the language lab

f. Feeling confused

g. Understanding other's ideas

h. Doing homework

i. A new job

j. Getting married

(Modeled after Niles et al 1965)

PART B This time two effects are listed in the left-hand column. From the right-hand column select the most probable causes for each effect. Write their numbers in the appropriate blank. Be ready to defend your choices.

Effects

A. A high rate of unemployment

_____

B. City slums

_____

Causes

1. Automation
2. Laziness
3. Increase in school dropouts
4. Landlords who disobey housing laws
5. Federal income taxes
6. Fewer jobs for unskilled workers
7. Upswing in juvenile delinquency
8. Poverty
9. Overcrowded living conditions
10. High-speed superhighways

(from *Tactics in Reading II*)

Sample Exercise G.16. Tracing Causes

Part 1
Presentation

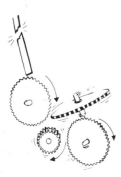

Study the following passage and the pictures which accompany it. Identify: a the problem, b the solution which has been adopted.

At 3.45 p.m. on August 6th 1976 Big Ben stopped working.

The engineers who repaired the clock believe that the breakdown was the result of metal fatigue. Metals deteriorate owing to repeated stresses above a certain critical value.

Part of the clock mechanism fractured. As a result, the speed of the gear wheels increased from about 1½ revolutions per minute to 16 000 rpm. The resulting centrifugal force threw pieces of the clock mechanism in all directions. It also damaged the mechanism which drives the clock's hands.

The metal fatigue had never been noticed, as fatigue cracks are invisible to the naked eye. The engineers have now fitted a device that will prevent the accident from happening again. Any increase in speed will cause a brake to be applied to the gear wheel. The engineers are confident that Big Ben will remain accurate and reliable for another 200 years.

Now answer these questions:
1 According to the engineers, what caused the clock to break down?
2 What general statement explains the occurrence of metal fatigue?

3   Why had the fatigue cracks never been noticed?

4   Complete the following diagram by studying the illustration of what happened:

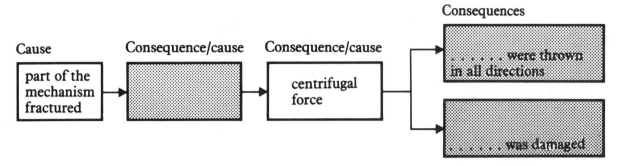

(from *Reading and Thinking in English*)

Sample Exercise G.17. (Beginning Level)

Read these paragraphs. Underline the signal words. Write the main ideas. Then fill in the tables below. Work with a partner.

A. A cold winter can cause serious problems for many people in Florida. The farmers grow oranges, and cold weather can result in many orange trees dying. A cold winter can also result in fewer tourists, so the bad weather can lead to problems for the people who own hotels and restaurants. And very cold weather can cause health problems for the old people who do not have enough heat in their homes.

Main idea:_____

————————— Causes —————————   ————————— Effects ———————

B. There are many different causes of car accidents in the United States. Sometimes accidents are caused by bad weather. Ice or snow make the roads dangerous. Accidents can also result from car problems. Even a flat tire can be serious. Bad roads also cause accidents, and bad drivers can cause them too. Drivers who fall asleep and drivers who drink alcohol cause many accidents in this country.

Main Idea:_____

————————— Causes —————————   ————————— Effects —————————

Sample Exercise G.18.

Write the topic for each paragraph. Underline the signal words. Write the causes and effects on the lines.

1

Most people do not think of coffee as a drug. But, in fact, it is a drug and it has important effects on your body. Some of the effects are good and some are not. Coffee can help you stay awake when you are driving or working. But it can also keep you awake at night when you want to sleep. Coffee makes some people feel more alive so they can work better. Other people feel too nervous when they drink coffee. After a large meal, coffee can help your stomach. But too much coffee can cause a stomachache.

Topic:_____

Causes	Signals	Effects
_____	_____	_____
_____	_____	_____
_____	_____	_____
_____	_____	_____
_____	_____	_____
_____	_____	_____

2

In the United States, poor city children are often ill because of their diet. Some children do not get enough food. Sometimes they do not get healthy food. Poor health is also caused by bad housing. The apartments may not have heat in the winter or fresh air in the summer. Poor health may also be the result of dirty water. Or it may be caused by crowded apartments and crowded schools.

Topic: _____

Causes	Signals	Effects
_____	_____	_____
_____	_____	_____
_____	_____	_____
_____	_____	_____
_____	_____	_____

(from *Reading Power*)

Sample Exercise G.19. Recognizing Cause-Effect Relationships in Longer Passages. (Advanced Level)

Directions: In this passage, you can find many cause-effect relationships. List them below, and then compare your work with another student's. Who found the most cause-effect relationships?

The Distribution of Land Animals

The distribution of land animals is affected by barriers to dispersal and the influence of man. After the Cenozoic period, 65 million years ago, the predominance of reptilian species came to an end. The mass extinctions of the dinosaurs marked the beginning of the predominance of mammals. Mammals occur in every habitable region on the globe. Their physiological composition is such that they are higly adaptable, a result of their homeothermy, fur, sweating, and panting. This allows mammals to establish colonies in a multitude of habitats. The number of habitable regions is now dwindling, however, due to the ever-increasing needs of *homo sapiens* for additional space and resources.

In the Holocene period, the mammal *homo sapiens* has affected other organisms more than any other creature has in the past. Many creatures have been introduced into new and distant lands through the agency of man. The addition to or the subsequent subtraction from (i.e. extinction) of a species to an area has at times been manipulated by the whim of man. The ramifications of man determining the distribution of species are only just beginning to be understood. Man has introduced animals of varying areas both deliberately and accidentally. Most have been tragic mistakes. The immigrant often enters an ideal environment, an environment which provides abundant food and few predators. Consequently, the population of the newly-established colony grows too quickly. The colonists become menaces and man then has to limit and reduce the increase in population by becoming an artificial pressure.

(E. Mikulecky 1984, used by permission)

What is the over-all cause? What is the over-all effect?

Cause:_____

Effect:_____

What is the main idea?_____

_____

_____

Cause-effect relationships you found in the passage:

1.

2.

3.

4.

Intensive Reading Lesson

The students should be assigned several different kinds of cause-effect passages from the newspaper or other sources. It is the group application of the pattern-recognition skill that will foster the transfer of the skill as a comprehension strategy to other situations.

Practice in Identifying Patterns

Once the students have worked with the four patterns, it is a good idea to assign several exercises which will give them paractice in identifying patterns and discriminating between them. This will allow them to develop the meta-cognitive skill of thinking in terms of patterns.

Sample Rationale

It is very important to know the overall pattern of the text when you read. But there are also many patterns inside the text. Almost every paragraph has a pattern. It is important to be able to recognize patterns when they are all mixed in together.

Sample Exercise G.20. Identifying Relationship Patterns (Intermediate Level)

1

Identify the relationship patterns in the following sentences. Look for word clues, and ALWAYS consider the sense of the sentence as a whole. In the blanks write TO if the relationship pattern in the sentence is TIME ORDER; CC if it is COMPARISON-CONTRAST; CE if it is CAUSE-EFFECT; SL if it is SIMPLE LISTING.

_____ 1. The tornado came from the collision of the warm low front with the cold high-pressure air mass.

_____ 2. After the tornado had passed, the city was deluged with torrential rains.

_____ 3. The downpour presented disaster victims with the additional problem of trying to keep dry.

_____ 4. Officials said that the storm was worse than any other disaster that had struck the area during the past fifty years.

_____ 5. There were not so many injuries as in the 1950 tornado, but the property damage was ten times as great.

_____ 6. Two hundred and fifty families were left homeless by the storm.

_____ 7. In recent months the city has had many troubles: record-breaking snows, high unemployment, a water shortage, a flu epidemic, and now a tornado.

_____ 8. The people have shown patience, courage, ingenuity, and a remarkable sense of humor.

_____ 9. The trouble seemed to inspire many people to behave unselfishly.

_____ 10. Although most citizens were too stunned to consider what had to be done, a few of the men began to organize volunteer clean-up crews.

2

Identify the relationship patterns in the following sentences. In the blanks write TO for TIME ORDER; CC for COMPARISON-CONTRAST; CE for CAUSE-EFFECT; or SL for SIMPLE LISTING.

_____ 1. He tried to remember all that the golf instructor had told him about the correct way to putt: interlocking grip, loose wrists, head down, eye upon the ball, knees together and slightly bent.

_____ 2. He sank nine out of ten putts; the weeks of practice had paid off.

_____ 3. That was more success than he usually had.

_____ 4. After finishing practice on the putting green, he stopped for a cold drink and then began working on his drive.

_____ 5. There was something wrong with his stance that made his ball slice wildly away toward the right.

_____ 6. Suddenly a bird started singing a cheerful tune much more persistent than his angry mutterings.

_____ 7. The unexpected sound made him forget his bad drive and take time to look around him.

_____ 8. He admired the gently rolling landscape, the blue sky with its soft white clouds, and the sparkle of the sun on the pond of the next water hole.

_____ 9. Two squirrels suddenly appeared, scurried toward a large oak tree, scrambled up its trunk, and after leaping about from branch to branch, settled on the lowest one and proceeded to scold him.

_____ 10. "So much noise," he commented dryly, "on such a quiet morning!"

When you identify common relationship patterns, you can put them to work for you as aids to remembering what you are reading. To do this:

If you recognize a time order pattern . . . ask yourself . . . In what order did these things happen?

If you recognize a comparison-contrast pattern . . . ask yourself . . . How are these things alike or different?

If you recognize a cause-effect pattern . . . ask yourself . . . How did these things result from or affect each other?

(from *Tactics in Reading III*)

Sample Exercise G.21. Anticipating Patterns

The clues given in the title or opening sentences of an article often help you to anticipate the predominant thought pattern of the entire article. In these cases, your awareness of the relationship of ideas and events will help you to recognize and remember the importance and meaning of the ideas and events emphasized by the author.

Assume that each of the numbered sentences in this exercise is the beginning sentence of a selection that you are about to read. What relationship pattern would you expect to find in the rest of the selection? If you think that the ideas and events following the opening sentence would be likely to be related by when they happen, write TO in the blank to the left of the sentence. Write CE if the clues point to a cause-effect relationship, CC if they indicate comparison-contrast, or SL if simple listing is indicated.

_____ 1. The success of the Firefall Hockey Team has apparently been dependent upon the health and morale of its team members.

_____ 2. Again and again throughout the season, the Adula basketball team has changed defeat to victory in the last few minutes of play.

_____ 3. The astronauts who spin around the earth in breath-taking exploits owe their comfort and safety to the ingenious minds and tireless efforts of a multitude of little-known men.

_____ 4. Whether you drive a plush-lined luxury car or a rattling jalopy, your automobile bears little resemblance to the vehicle that will take commuters to and from their work in the future.

_____ 5. It was more than twenty years ago that Felix Juarez first dreamed of a bridge across the Santos River, and now, after years of trying to convince others of the need for such a bridge, he is finally seeing his dream come true in concrete and graceful steel arches.

_____ 6. When the American taxpayer mournfully totals up his taxes for a year, he is likely to be quite unaware of the many services for which his tax dollar is spent.

_____ 7. Many products that were once considered to be luxuries are now thought of as downright necessities.

_____ 8. An examination of the history of our republic furnishes ample evidence that the life and growth of a democratic society is dependent upon the life and growth of its educational opportunities.

_____ 9. Of all the plays that Joseph Lockington wrote, "The Fifth Banjo String" is by far his best.

_____ 10. The modern American housewife is expected to be an expert in a great many areas besides cooking and laundry.

(from *Tactics in Reading III*)

Sample Exercise G.22. Identifying Patterns

Directions: Here are four paragraphs about Sir Isaac Newton. Read each paragraph, and then choose one sentence from the extra sentences below and write the letter for that sentence next to the paragraph in which it would fit best. One of the sentences will not be used.

Paragraph 1

Sir Isaac Newton worked on many important scientific problems. First, there was his development of the laws of motion. He also made important discoveries about optics and the nature of color. His other work included ideas about astronomy, chemistry, and logic. And finally, he produced the *Principia*, a book which explained his law of universal gravitation.

Paragraph 2

Isaac Newton was born in England in 1642. He went to Trinity College, Cambridge University, in 1661 at the age of 18. In 1665, the plague swept through England, and Newton left school and returned to his family home in Woolsthorpe. It was there that he began most of his best work. He published his famous book, the *Principia*, in 1682. And in 1699 he was made the director of the English Mint. Sir Isaac Newton died in 1727 and he is buried in Westminster Abbey.

Paragraph 3

Although the two men were both geniuses, Isaac Newton and Albert Einstein have very little else in common. True, they both did their most important and famous work before the age of 26. But there are great differences between them. "Proper behavior" was most important to Newton, while Einstein liked to be different. Newton spent his later years working for the government, while Einstein spent his entire life doing science.

Paragraph 4

Newton did most of his best work during his stay in Woolsthrope from 1665 to 1668. Many writers have tried to find out what caused him to produce all of those great ideas in such a short time. Was it the peace and quiet of the small town that caused his creative powers to increase? The causes may never be known, but the effects of Newton's genius are still felt today.

Extra Sentences

1. Some people think that a falling apple caused Newton to think of the law of universal gravitation.
2. Present-day physicists have discovered limits to the mechanical universe which Newton described.
3. In addition, he invented differential and integral calculus.
4. They say Isaac Newton never smiled, but Albert Einstein had a great sense of humor.
5. In fact, by age 26, he had already completed most of his best scientific work.

(B. Mikulecky 1984)

Notes: **1.** The teacher's objective is to help students develop a schema of textual patterns by giving them the opportunity to engage intensively in several different patterns. The sample exercises focus on four of the most common patterns, but they by no means exhaust all of the possibilities. Other relationship patterns include argumentation, problem/solution, climax (with most important or greatest idea at the end), classification, and definition. Teachers of science, social science, psychology, and math will undoubtedly think of other relationship patterns which will be useful for their students.

2. As we know, patterns of textual organization are not always signaled lexically; instead, they are very subtly shown by the content and the overall organization of the text. More advanced students (in other words, those whose language knowledge is sufficient to handle such texts) can benefit from practice with exercises which highlight strategies for recognizing organizational patterns when no lexical signals are given.

H. SKIMMING AND SUMMARIZING

Skimming

Skimming is very fast-paced reading. Effective skimming requires the reader to be able to process a text rapidly at many levels in order to get an overall picture of it. About 800 words per minute is considered a good skimming rate (Fry 1978).

Skimming is different from scanning, another fast-paced reading skill. Scanning is useful for finding specific pieces of information from a text, i.e., a phone number in a directory, a word in the dictionary, or a birthdate in a biographical description. But skimming is more comprehensive: effective skimming requires knowledge of textual organization, awareness of lexical clues to point of view, the ability to infer main ideas, and many other advanced reading skills.

Skimming may seem similar to previewing, but they are done for a different purpose. The reader previews to get a glimpse of the contents of a text before reading. But the reader *skims* to obtain an overview of the form and contents of a text, including such information as the writer's main point, style, focus, point of view, the overall organization of the material, and how the text relates to the needs, background knowledge, and interests of the reader. Armed with this information, the reader can decide how much more thoroughly a text should be read.

Sometimes skimming is all that is necessary to obtain the information the reader wants (as in skimming a newspaper or magazine article). Sometimes, the reader skims in order to decide whether or not to read a text thoroughly, or to review a text already read.

In order to skim, the reader has to be capable of quickly seeing the skeleton which underlies the text. It is easier to do that if the reader is aware of how texts are organized (for example, that, in English, the main point is usually stated at the beginning of a paragraph, section, or chapter). The reader should also be familiar with the important clues which are represented by differences in size and style of type in the text, as well as the lexical items used for signaling relationships between ideas and the vocabulary of textual cohesion. This is knowledge which most second language learners need to acquire before they can skim effectively. Therefore, it may be a good idea to delay a focus on the skimming skill until second language readers and other limited English proficient students have developed the ability to apply many of the reading skills presented in this book.

As with any of the skills, the students should be aware of the practical reasons for skimming. A discussion of questions such as those in the Sample Rationale (below) will help the students understand why they need to learn to skim.

Sample Rationale

What should you do?

1. You have three different books about the same subject, and you need to decide which one to read.

2. You need some special information and you have found many books about the same topic. You need to find out which books have the information you need.

3. You would like to know a little about an event, but you do not have time to read a whole article about it.

4. You read a book a few years ago, and now you want to talk about it with someone.

5. You have a few books about a subject, and you want to find out each author's main point or opinion. Do you have to read the books all the way through again?

6. You are at the book store, looking for a good book to read for pleasure. How can you find out if you will enjoy a book?

The answer to all six situations is the same:

You should skim.

When you skim, you read very fast: about 800 words per minute! You do not read very many words. You read to find out what the text is about, how it is organized, the author's point of view, and the author's approach to the topic.

Skimming is an important skill because you can save time; you can quickly decide what to read and what not to read.

Sample Exercise H.1. How to Skim

Shown on the following page is a view of how you might skim an article. Notice that you read all of the first and second paragraphs to get an overview. By the third of fourth paragraph you must begin to leave out material; read only key sentences and phrases to get the main ideas and a few of the details. Note also that, since final paragraphs often summarize, it may be worth while to read them more fully.

Skimming must be done "against the clock." That is, you must try to go as fast as you possibly can while leaving out large chunks of material. Be careful to avoid getting interested in the story since this might slow you down and cause you to read unnecessary detail. Skimming is work. It is done when you do not have much time and when you wish to cover material at the fastest possible rate.

Usually the first paragraph will be read at average speed all the way through. It often contains an introduction or overview of what will be talked about.

Sometimes, however, the second paragraph contains the introduction or overview. In the first paragraph the author might just be "warming up" or saying something clever to attract attention.

Reading a third paragraph completely might be unnecessary but ....

the main idea is usually contained in the opening sentence .... topic sentence ....

Besides the first sentence the reader should get some but not all the detail from the rest of the paragraph ....

names ....
....
dates ....
....

This tells you nothing ....
....

.... hence sometimes the main idea is in the middle or at the end of the paragraph.

Some paragraphs merely repeat ideas ....

Occasionally the main idea can't be found in the opening sentence. The whole paragraph must then be read.

Then leave out a lot of the next paragraph .... to make up time ....

Remember to keep up a very fast rate .... 800 w.p.m. ....

Don't be afraid to leave out half or more of each paragraph ....

Don't get interested and start to read everything .... skimming is work ....

....

Lowered comprehension is expected ....

50% .... not too low ....

Skimming practice makes it easier ....

gain confidence ....

Perhaps you won't get anything at all from a few paragraphs .... don't worry ....

Skimming has many uses ....
reports ....
newspapers ....
.... supplementary text ....

The ending paragraphs might be read more fully as often they contain a summary.

Remember that the importance of skimming is to get only the author's main ideas at a very fast speed.

(from *Skimming and Scanning*)

Sample Exercise H.2. (Beginning Level)

A Busy Student

Tomiko is happy to be a student in New York. She is studying English at Columbia University. She plans to finish her English course in June. Then she will work on her master's degree at New York University.

Tomiko likes the many beautiful buildings in New York. xxxxxxxxxxxxx
xxxxxxxxxxxxxxxxxxxxxxxxxxxxxxxxxxxxxxxxxxxxxxxxxxxxxxxxxxxxxxxxxxxxxx
xxxxxxxxxxxxxxxxxxxxxxxxxxxxxxxxxxxxxxxxxxxxxxxxxxxxxxxxxxxxxxxxxxxxxx

She also likes the people in New York. xxxxxxxxxxxxxxxxxxxxxxxxxxxx
xxxxxxxxxxxxxxxxxxxxxxxxxxxxxxxxxxxxxxxxxxxxxxxxxxxxxxxxxxxxxxxxxxxxxx
xxxxxxxxxxxxxxxxxxxxxxxxxxxxxxxxxxxxxxxxxxxxxxxxxxxxxxxxxxxxxxxxxxxxxx

Best of all, Tomiko loves the theaters in New York. xxxxxxxxxxxxxxxxx
xxxxxxxxxxxxxxxxxxxxxxxxxxxxxxxxxxxxxxxxxxxxxxxxxxxxxxxxxxxxxxxxxxxxxx
xxxxxxxxxxxxxxxxxxxxxxxxxxxxxxxxxxxxxxxxxxxxxxxxxxxxxxxxxxxxxxxxxxxxxx
xxxxxxxxxxxxxxxxxxxxxxxxxxxxxxxxxxxxxxxxxxxxxxxxxxxxxxxxxxxxxxxxxxxxxx

Tomiko is far from her home in Japan. But she is not sad. xxxxxxxxxxx
xxxxxxxxxxxxxxxxxxxxxxxxxxxxxxxxxxxxxxxxxxxxxxxxxxxxxxxxxxxxxxxxxxxxxx
xxxxxxxxxxxxxxxxxxxxxxxxxxxxxxxxxxxxxxxxxxxxxxxxxxxxxxxxxxxxxxxxxxxxxx
xxxxxxxxxxxxxxxxxxxxxxxxxxxxxxxxx . She is very busy and happy in New York.
Circle the best answer. Don't look back at the passage.

1. This passage is about
   a. an American student in New York.
   b. a Japanese student in New York.
   c. a Japanese student in Japan.
   d. a Japanese man studying in New York.

2. Tomiko is
   a. unhappy.
   b. happy.
   c. lonely.
   d. not busy.

3. She goes to plays in
   a. large theaters.
   b. small theatres.
   c. New York.
   d. all of the above.

4. Tomiko has
   a. few interests.
   b. few friends.
   c. many interests.
   d. nothing to do.

Now read the whole passage.

A Busy Student

Tomiko is happy to be a student in New York. She is studying English at Columbia University. She plans to finish her English course in June. Then she will work on her master's degree at New York University.

Tomiko likes the many beautiful buildings in New York. In fact, she plans to become an architect. Then she can build great buildings, too.

Tomiko also likes the people in New York City. There are many different kinds of people. They speak many languages. Tomiko has made new friends from other countries.

Best of all, Tomiko loves the theatres in New York. She goes to plays almost every week. Sometimes the plays are in theaters on Broadway. Sometimes the plays are in small theaters in other parts of the city.

Tomiko is far from her home in Japan. But she is not sad. She goes to classes every day. She visits her friends. She goes to see new places. And she attends many plays. She is very busy and happy in New York.

How many did you answer correctly? _____

You can learn a lot about a passage if you read just a few important sentences.

(from *Reading Power*)

Sample Exercise H.3.

1

Specific aim: To train the students to skim through a
                   text.
Skills involved: Predicting.
                   Anticipating.
Why?   One way of skimming through a text is to
                   look at the beginning of each paragraph.
                   The very first words used often give us
                   precious clues to the discourse function as
                   well as to the contents of what follows.

The title, the first sentence and the first words of each
paragraph of an article have been given below. They should be
enough to give you an idea of the contents of the article. Tick
the boxes corresponding to the points that you think are
mentioned.

Nuclear cloud spreads

PENNSYLVANIA came close to a nuclear catastrophe yesterday as the nuclear power station at Harrisburg started releasing radio-active steam into the air.

It all began ....

....

The probable cause ....

....

As in the 1950 catastrophe in

The situation today is still .....

....

However ....

....

Officials said ....

....

This happened just as ....

....

The new film describes ....

....

Let us hope ....

....

The article tells us/mentions:

no evidence
perhaps
yes

☐ ☐ ☐ other catastrophes of that kind have happened before
☐ ☐ ☐ why this accident happened
☐ ☐ ☐ the danger is now over
☐ ☐ ☐ the opinion of the workers in the station
☐ ☐ ☐ the opinion of the authorities
☐ ☐ ☐ a description of the accident
☐ ☐ ☐ a film was made of this accident
☐ ☐ ☐ a film about a nuclear catastrophe has just come out
☐ ☐ ☐ it should be a warning to all governments
☐ ☐ ☐ it is the first incident of this kind
☐ ☐ ☐ the situation should improve soon
☐ ☐ ☐ what the other dangers of a nuclear station are

2

Specific aim:	To train the students to skim through a text.
Skills involved:	Predicting. Anticipating.
Why?	The aim of this exercise is to encourage the weaker students who tend to read slowly and never skim through a text because they think there is too much they do not understand. The idea here is to show them that even a few words understood here and there can be enough to understand what the passage is about. In fact, it is what often happens when we run our eyes over a text to get the gist of it.

You are skimming through an article in which most of the words
are unknown to you. Here are the ones you can understand, however:
professor
Institute of Biochemistry
hard-working man
results of experiments
published
confession
invention
different results
fraud
regrets it

Can you guess, from these few words, if the article is about
☐ a well-known professor who has just published his confessions
☐ a scientist who has admitted inventing the results of his
experiments
☐ a scientist who has killed himself because he couldn't get the
same results as everybody else
☐ a scientist who regrets the publication of the results of his
experiments

(From *Developing Reading Skills*)

Sample Exercise H.4. Skimming a Newspaper Article (Beginning Level)

Skim this newspaper article. You should finish in less than 60 seconds. Then answer the questions.

A New Drug for Heart Attacks

Doctors may now be able to stop many heart attacks. An important new study reports that doctors have a new drug. This drug is called TPA. It may be better than any other heart drug.

Many doctors now use a drug called Streptokinase. But this drug sometimes causes problems for patients. It can even cause bleeding in the brain. Some doctors do not use streptokinase. Streptokinase can save about $\frac{1}{3}$ of the people with heart attacks. But TPA will save about $\frac{2}{3}$. This means many people. About 1.5 million Americans have heart attacks every year.

One reason TPA can help more people is because of time. This new drug is easier and faster to use. It will give doctors more time in hospitals. Then they can study the problem well. People with heart problems can also keep some TPA at home. When a heart attack starts, they can take some TPA right away. Then they will have time to get to the hospital. This is important because about 860,000 people in the United States die before they get to the hospital.

There is another reason why TPA is good news for people with heart attacks. According to the study, it is much safer. It does not cause other problems like streptokinase. TPA works only on the heart. It does not have an effect on the blood or cause bleeding, like streptokinase.

Doctors plan to do more studies about TPA. They need to test this new drug on many more people with heart attacks. But in a few years, many doctors and hospitals will probably start using this exciting new drug.

1. The new drug is
   a. the same as streptokinase.
   b. better than streptokinase.
   c. called streptokinase.
   d. bad for people with heart attacks.

2. The study says that TPA
   a. is safer and faster than the old drug.
   b. is very dangerous.
   c. slower and harder to use than the old drug.
   d. causes many problems.

3. This new drug may mean
   a. more people will die from heart attacks.
   b. the same number of people will die from heart attacks.
   c. fewer people will die from heart attacks.
   d. no one will die from heart attacks.

(from *Reading Power*)

Summarizing

Although some people do not realize it, summarizing is an important reading skill. When readers summarize, they demonstrate their comprehension of the text. Summary-writing requires the reader to apply many of the skills which have been described in this book. Also, the act of writing a summary reinforces interactive top-down and bottom-up modes of processing, and it makes readers aware of their own understanding of a text. And, importantly, summarizing forces readers to be concsiously aware of the strategies they apply for comprehending.

Brown and Day (1980) developed six rules for summarizing:

1. Delete unnecessary material — information that is trivial.
2. Delete material that is important but redundant.
3. Substitute a superordinate term for a list of items. If a text contains a list such as chair, table, desk, substitute the word *furniture*.
4. Substitute an encompassing action for a list of subcomponents of that action. For example. *John went to London* may be substituted for *John left the house. He went to the train station. He bought a ticket.*
5. Select a topic sentence. The topic sentence, if there is one, usually is the author's summary of the paragraph . . . . . .
6. If there is no topic sentence, invent your own.

(Quoted in McNeil 1987:157)

If students follow these steps, they are likely to produce a good summary. But one step should be added which would help readers consolidate their understanding.

7. Determine the overall pattern of organization of the text. Is it a comparison? A choronology? An analysis of a process? An explanation of causes and effects? An argument?

Day's study of instruction in summarizing (1980) showed that junior college students can be trained to produce good summaries by following the rules above, with explicit instruction and modeling at each step. Donant (McNeil and Donant 1982), working with fifth-grade children, also demonstrated that explicit teaching of such rules was effective in training the children to write good summaries and to better comprehend what they read.

Sample Rationale

When you read something that you want to remember, it is a good idea to write a summary. A summary includes the important ideas, but it is often only 10% as long as the original text. If you can find the topic sentence and the pattern of organization, you can learn to summarize.

Follow these steps:

1. Read the passage through.

2. Find the topic sentence. If there is no topic sentence, write one of your own.

3. Decide on the over-all pattern of organization.

4. Cross out all the unimportant information, ideas that are not connected to the topic. Also, cross out ideas that are repeated.

5. If there is a list of details, think of a word which names them all. For example, dog, cat, horse, elephant can be crossed out and the word *animals* can be used instead.

6. If many actions are listed, think of a word which names them all. For example, Andrew took the meat and vegetables out of the refrigerator. He got out a pan. He chopped up the food. You can put these together as, *Andrew cooked dinner*.

When you write a summary, you have a chance to apply many reading skills that you have learned, and you can find out if you really understood what you read.

Sample Exercise H.5. Summarizing a Paragraph

Directions: Part I. Read this paragraph and the summary below. Notice how much of the paragraph was left out of the summary.

Shopping malls have produced a revolution in American shopping and living habits in just 37 years. Before 1950, there were no malls, and now almost every small city has at least one. In fact, shopping malls have become a part of American society and many people think of them as social centers. In a way, malls have taken the place of Main Street. All of the shops and most of the services which were once spread out over several city blocks are now in one place at the mall. Busy householders can save time by doing their shopping at the mall. And people young and old, with time on their hands, often say "Let's go to the mall!"

Summary: *Shopping malls have changed the United States and have become a part of American society in just 37 years.*

Directions: Part II. Summarize these paragraphs. Follow the six summarizing steps. Compare your summary with another student's. Are they the same?

1. Every mall has its own atmosphere, but there are many similarities. One could go to a mall in an unfamiliar city and feel quite at home. You can always find most of the following: a Woolworth's or other variety shop, a pharmacy, a toy store, a book store, clothing shops for all ages, sporting goods shops, jewelry shops, shoe shops, a bank, and places to eat. These businesses are all under one roof. Some malls are enclosed so that shoppers never have to go

outdoors once they get to the mall. Others have the doors to the shops on the outside of the mall. Every mall is surrounded by a large parking area.

Summary:

2. The socioeconomic class of the nearby residents is reflected in the shopping mall. In a poor rural town in southern Maine, for example, a typical mall usually has a supermarket, a pizza parlor, a book and gift shop, a laundromat, and a bank. The shops are all on one level, and the interior of the enclosed mall is plain and undecorated. In contrast, a large mall in a wealthy suburb of Chicago is two stories tall and houses about 50 business, ranging from small specialty shops to large luxury department stores. The interior of the mall soars twice as tall as the shops, and the roof is made of glass. There is live music in the evening, and trees and fountains are located in central areas. But these malls are alike because they both allow people to shop American-style: at the mall.

Summary:

Intensive Reading Lesson

If the students have been trained in all of the skills discussed in this book, an intensive reading lesson at this point can be used to apply any of the skills which are relevant to the text the class reads.

Appendix

1. Brief Review of Methodology Suggested in This Book

It is suggested that teachers focus on specific reading skills and that they work to make students consciously aware of their application of the skills for improving comprehension. Further, students should be given every possible opportunity to work interactively and often collaboratively on learning and applying reading skills. This is recommended because it fosters the articulation and acquisition of new ways of thinking about text (Hoffman and Heath 1986) and acknowledges the social nature of learning (Tierney and Cunningham 1984:640).

2. Teachers Reading Aloud

Teachers should read aloud to their students for several reasons.

First, students can benefit from hearing good reading modeled for them.

Second, students can hear some of the stories and tales which might be more difficult for them to read, due to dialect and complicated paragraphs. (This is where we can introduce Mark Twain and Charles Dickens!)

Third, students who would not normally select fiction might be tempted once they experienced it.

Fourth, teachers can read poetry to their students simply for the sound of the language.

Fifth, teachers can model a way of reading stories which develops literate skills, interpolating elaborative questions along the way.

Sixth, students will have a shared literacy event which they can discuss.

3. Students Reading Aloud

Teachers should take care to use student oral reading productively.

First, students concentrate on pronunciation when they read aloud. Therefore, they cannot concentrate on meaning or be expected to answer comprehension questions after reading aloud.

Second, many students feel awkward reading aloud in front of the class. Erickson (1987) describes this a "public display of incompetence," truly a humiliating situation.

Third, reading aloud is effective when it is done for authentic reasons. Therefore, certain kinds of reading aloud work well, including choral reading, jazz chants, and plays. Other kinds of authentic reading aloud include group reports to the class, reading students' own writing to a peer group for feedback, reading a short segment of text to prove a point, or reading for pronunciation practice.

4. More about Cloze

How a cloze passage is constructed depends in part on how the teacher intends to use it. To construct a cloze passage which can be used for determining the student's ability to comprehend a particular text:

a. Select a text suitable for the language level of your students. If you use a text which has already been "graded" (assigned a level of difficulty), the results will be more useful.

b. Decide on a deletion rate. Difficulty increases with the frequency of deletions.

c. Leave the first sentence intact.

d. Delete every *n*th word (10th, 7th, 5th). Leave a blank of exactly the same size for every missing word.

Using a conventional cloze instrument:

a. A short introductory exercise should be used before students are asked to do a cloze exercise for the first time. They should be told to read *past* the blanks before trying to fill them in. The class should discuss the exercise and students should feel comfortable with the process before a cloze test is administered.

b. Students should be told to try to think of the exact word which the author used in each space. Only the exact words will be scored as correct.

c. Cloze scoring when the exact word is required:

      61% or more correct   = independent reading level
      41–60% correct   = instructional reading level
      40% or less correct   = frustration reading level.

Cloze exercises are often used as instructional devices as well, and are frequently used for training students in how to guess word meanings from context.

Variations on the conventional cloze passage:

a. Present the passage with conventional deletions, but allow any acceptable word as correct.

b. Multiple-choice cloze (Olsen, 1982; Bensoussan, 1983) for testing reading comprehension.

Example:

There was a table set out under a tree in front of the house, and the March Hare and the Hatter were	Circle the Answer
having tea at (1) them. (2) it. (3) once. (4) her. A	1 2 3 4
Dormouse was sitting between them, fast (1) runner, (2) quiet, (3) eating, (4) asleep, and the other two	1 2 3 4
were resting their (1) selves (2) comfortably (3) elbows (4) hand on it and talking over its head.	1 2 3 4

c. Matching cloze (Olsen, 1982)

Example:

A girl named Jane lived in a _____ in the	Choose a word
village. She _____ there with her mother,	day
	father
_____, and two brothers. One _____	house
	lived
they went to the _____ to fish.	sea

d. The C-text (Raatz and Klein-Braley, 1984)

"Every second word is deleted. However, in order to ensure that solution is possible at all, we leave the first half of the deleted word standing. If the word has an odd number of letters, we delete exactly half the word plus half a letter. If the word consists only of one letter, then this word is ignored in the counting, and half the following word is deleted . . . . . Only entirely correct restorations are counted as right."

See Sample Exercise D.7 on page 70.

e.   You can construct a "rational" cloze test by deleting specific words or types of words. In a pilot test of such a rational cloze test, Mikulecky and Bensousson deleted words which were signals to text cohesion in order to test macro-level comprehension. Here is a short portion of the test:

There are many ways to travel: by land, by sea, and by air. People have been traveling by land and sea for many centuries. But it is (1) _____ that people have been able to travel (2) _____. This is because air travel is (3) _____ man-made techniques and inventions.

Answer Sheet

Circle the word which best fits the text.

	A	B	C	D
1.	rather strange	also true	a long time	only lately
2.	by air	on foot	by water	on horseback
3.	made difficult by	changing	the result of	the reason for

5. What are Schemata?

According to Rumelhart and Ortony (1977:101),

Schemata are data structures for representing the general concepts stored in memory. They exist for generalized concepts underlying objects, situations, events, sequences of events, actions, and sequences of actions. Schemata are not atomic. A schema contains, as part of its specification, the network of interrelationships that is believed to generally hold among the constituents of the concept in question. Schemata, in some sense, represent stereotypes of these concepts. Although it oversimplifies the matter somewhat, it may be useful to think of a schema as analogous to a play with the internal structure of the schema corresponding to the script of the play. A schema is related to a particular instance of the concept that it represents in much the same way that a play is related to a particular enactment of the play.

Here are some examples of schemata discussed by Winograd (1977:75-76):

a. Schemata concerned with the subject matter of discourse

Events at a birthday party
Eating in a restaurant
Taking a bus
Getting an ice cream cone
Breaking some physical object

Other schemata of this type may be associated with animate or inanimate objects

An elephant
A home
A flush toilet
The structure of a device being worked on
Spatial representations, such as the way people describe apartment layouts.

b. Schemata involved in communication situations.

Distinguishing between
    "And then he told me I was wrong."
        and
    "And then he told me, 'I was wrong.'
and knowing who the "he" and "I" are.

c. Schemata involved in discourse situations

Interpersonal schemata: conventions for participating in the communication: "How do you do?"

Rhetorical schemata: conventions for laying out a reasoning sequence: i.e., language signals such as *therefore, because, so*, etc. and parallel sentences in sequences such as:

"He must be here. His light is still on."

Schemata for narratives: conventions for stringing together a sequence of statements into a coherent text. For example, simple story forms and conventions, such as mysteries, children's tales, flashbacks, resolutions, etc.

Schemata for structures of oral discourse rules, the uses of language and reading and writing (McNeil 1987:9).

6. The Reading Skills Not Discussed in This Book

In Part II, 24 reading skills were listed. They are all important. For the purposes of this book, skills were selected which are most needed by ESL/EFL and other non-"mainstream" students. Exercises focusing on the other skills can be found in many texts.

However, the author hopes that the readers of this book have come to understand that creating exercise sequences tailored for specific classes is the most effective way to teach reading skills. In designing a sequence of lessons, just follow these guiding principles:

a. Select a skill.
b. Locate, write, or adapt a sequence of exercises, beginning at a very simple level. Make the sequence developmental.

c. Think of a way of introducing the skill to your students which makes clear to them the significance of this skill for reading improvement. (That's your rationale.)

d. Be sure to provide opportunities for the students to apply the new skills in Intensive Reading Lessons based on passages which are interesting, relevant, and accessible. You are the best judge of that. A passage from a reader is fine, if it contains information which your class is really interested in.

FEEDBACK

The author would like your response to this approach to teaching reading. After you have tried it, please write!

Beatrice Mikulecky
c/o Addison-Wesley Publishing Company
World Language Division
Reading, MA U.S.A. 01867

Bibliography

References

Alderson, J. C. 1984. Reading in a foreign language: a reading problem or a language problem? In J. C. Alderson and A. H. Urquhart (eds.), *Reading in a Foreign Language.* New York: Longman.

Baldauf, R. B. and Propst, I. K. 1979. Using matching cloze tests for elementary ESL students. *The Reading Teacher*, Vol. 32:683–690.

Bamford, J. 1984. Extensive Reading By Means of Graded Readers. *Reading in a Foreign Language* Vol. 2, #2.

Beck, I. L. and McKeown, M. G. 1986. Instructional Research in Reading: A Retrospective. In J. Orasanu (ed.) *Reading Comprehension: From Research to Practice.* Hillsdale, NJ: Lawrence Erlbaum Associates.

Bensoussan, M. 1983. Multiple-choice modification of the cloze procedure using word-length and sentence-length blanks. *Foreign Language Annals* Vol. 16(3):189–198.

Berkhoff, N. and Greenbaum, J. 1983. *Advanced Comprehension Techniques.* Jerusalem: The Hebrew University.

Besnier, N. 1986. Spoken and Written Language Differences in a Restricted Literacy Setting. Paper presented at the 11th Annual Boston University Conference on Language Development, October 17–19, 1986. Boston, MA.

Bransford, J. D. and Johnson, M. K. 1972. Contextual Prerequisites for Understanding: Some Investigations of Comprehension and Recall. *Journal of Verbal Learning and Verbal Behavior* Vol. 11, 717–726.

Brown, A. L. 1978. Knowing When, Where, and How to Remember: A Problem of Metacognition. In R. Glaser (ed.), *Advances In Instructional Psychology.* Hillsdale, NJ: Lawrence Erlbaum Associates.

———— 1980. Metacognitive development and reading. In R. J. Spiro, B. C. Bruce, and W. F. Brewer (eds.). *Theoretical Issues in Reading Comprehension.* Hillsdale, NJ: Lawrence Erlbaum Associates.

Brown, A. L., Armbruster, B. B., and Baker, L. 1986. The Role of Metacognition in Reading and Studying. In J. Orasanu, (ed.), *Reading Comprehension: From Research to Practice.* Hillsdale, NJ: Lawrence Erlbaum Associates.

Brown, A. L. and Day, J. 1983. Macrorules for summarizing texts: The development of Expertise. *Journal of Verbal Learning and Verbal Behavior* Vol. 22.

Brown, D. S. 1988. *A World of Books: An annotated reading list for ESL/EFL students.* Second edition, revised. Washington: TESOL.

Carrell, P. L. 1984. The effects of rhetorical organization on ESL readers. *TESOL Quarterly* Vol. 18, #3.

———— 1985. Facilitating ESL Reading by Teaching Text Structure. *TESOL Quarterly* Vol. 19, #4.

———— 1987. Content and Formal Schemata in ESL Reading. *TESOL Quarterly* Vol. 21, #3.

———— 1987. Text as Interaction: Some implications of text analysis and reading research for ESL composition. In U. Connor and R. Kaplan, (eds.) *Writing Across Languages: Analysis of L2 Texts.* Reading MA: Addison-Wesley Publishing Company.

Carroll, J. G., Davies, P., and Richman, B. 1971. *The American Heritage Word Frequency Book.* Boston: Houghton-Mifflin.

Casanave, C. P. 1988. Adding communication to the ESL reading class. *TESOL Newsletter* Vol. XII(3).

Cates, G. T. and Swaffar, J. K. 1979. *Language in Education: Theory and Practice #20 — Reading in a Second Language*. Washington, DC: Center for Applied Linguistics

Cazden, C. 1987. The Myth of Autonomous Text. Paper presented at the 12th Annual Boston University Conference on Language Development, October 23–25, 1987. Boston, MA.

Christison, M. and Krahnke, K. 1986. Student Perceptions of Academic Language Study. *TESOL Quarterly* Vol. 20, #1.

Clark, D. F. and Nation, L. 1980. Guessing the Meaning of Words from Context: Strategy and Techniques. *System* Vol. 8, #3.

Clarke, M. 1979. Reading in Spanish and English. *Language Learning* Vol. 29:121–150.

Clyne, M. 1980. Writing, testing and culture. *The Secondary Teacher* Vol. 11:13–16.

Coady, J. 1979. A Psycholinguistic Model of the ESL Reader. In R. Mackay, B. Barkman, and R. Jordan (eds.), *Reading in a Second Language: Hypotheses, Organization and Practice*. Rowley, MA: Newbury House Publishers.

Collins, A. and Smith, E. 1980. *Teaching the Process of Reading Comprehension* (Tech. Rep. No. 982) Urbana: University of Illinois, Center for the Study of Reading.

Connor, U. and Kaplan, R.(eds.), 1987. *Writing Across Languages: Analysis of L2 Text*. Reading, MA: Addison-Wesley Publishing Company.

Cook-Gumperz, J. (ed.). 1986. *The Social Construction of Literacy*. Cambridge: Cambridge University Press.

Cooper, C. R. and Petrosky, A. R. 1976. A Psycholinguistic View of the Fluent Reading Process. *Journal of Reading* Vol. 20.

Cooper, M. 1984. Linguistic Competence of Practiced and Unpracticed Non-native Readers of English. In J. C. Anderson and A. H. Urquhart, (eds.). *Reading in a Foreign Language*. New York: Longman.

Crow, J. and Quigley, J. 1985. A Semantic Field Approach to Passive Vocabulary Acquisition for Reading Comprehension. *TESOL Quarterly* Vol. 19, #3.

Cziko, G. 1978. Differences in first- and second-language reading: the use of syntactic, semantic, and discourse constraints. *Canadian Modern Language Review* Vol. 34:473–489.

D'Andrade, R. 1981. The Cultural Part of Cognition. *Cognitive Science* Vol. 5:179–195.

de Castell, S., Luke, A., and Egan, K. (eds.), 1986. *Literacy, Society, and Schooling: A Reader*. Cambridge: Cambridge University Press.

Dubin, F., Eskey, D., and Grabe, W. (eds.), 1986. *Teaching Second Language Reading for Academic Purposes*. Reading, MA: Addison-Wesley Publishing Company.

Edelsky, C. 1986. *Writing in a Bilingual Program: Habia una vez*. Norwood, NJ: Ablex Publishing Company.

Eggington, W. G., 1987. Written Academic Discourse in Korean: Implications for Effective Communication. In U. Connor and R. Kaplan, (eds.). *Writing Across Languages: Analysis of L2 Text*. Reading, MA: Addison-Wesley Publishing Company.

Erickson, F. 1987. Paper presented at the 12th Annual Boston University Conference on Language Development. October 23–25, 1987. Boston, MA.

Eskey, D. 1973. A model program for teaching advanced reading to students of English as a foreign language. *Language Learning* Vol. 23(2):169–184.

———— 1986. Theoretical Foundations. In F. Dubin, D. Eskey and W. Grabe, (eds.). *Teaching Second Language Reading for Academic Purposes*. Reading, MA: Addison-Wesley Publishing Company.

Flavell, J. H. and Wellman, H. J. 1977. Metamemory. In R. V. Kail and J. W. Hagen (eds.), *Perspectives on the development of memory and cognition*. Hillsdale, NJ: Lawrence Erlbaum Associates.

Freebody, P. and Anderson, R. C. 1983. Effects of vocabulary difficulty, text cohesion, and schema availability on reading comprehension. *Reading Research Quarterly* Vol. 18.

Gee, J. P. 1985. The Narrativization of Experience in the Oral Style. *Journal of Education* Vol. 167, #1.

———— 1986. Orality and Literacy: From *The Savage Mind* to *Ways With Words*. *TESOL Quarterly* Vol. 20, #4.

Gipe, J. P. 1978–79. Investigating techniques for teaching word meanings. *Reading Research Quarterly* Vol. 14 (4):624–644.

Goodman, K. S. 1970. Reading: A Psycholinguistic Guessing Game. In H. Singer and R. B. Ruddell (eds.) *Theoretical Models and Processes in Reading*. Newark, DE: International Reading Association.

———— 1971. Psycholinguistic Universals in the Reading Process. In P. Pimsleur and T. Quinn (eds.) *The Psychology of Second Language Learning*. Cambridge: Cambridge University Press.

Grabe. W. 1986. The Transition from Theory to Practice in Teaching Reading. In F. Dubin, D. E. Eskey and W. Grabe (eds.), *Teaching Second Language Reading for Academic Purposes*. Reading, MA: Addison-Wesley Publishing Co.

Graff, H. 1979. *The Literacy Myth: Literacy and Social Structure in the 19th Century City*. New York: Academic Press.

Grellet, F. 1981. *Developing Reading Skills: A Practical Guide to Reading Comprehension Exercises*. Cambridge: Cambridge University Press.

Haber, L. R. and Haber, R. N. 1981. Perceptual Processes in Reading: An Analysis-by-Synthesis Model. In F. Pirozzolo and M. Wittrock, (eds.), *Neuropsychological and Cognitive Processes in Reading*. New York: Academic Press.

Hall, W. S., White, T. G. and Guthrie, L. 1986. Skilled Reading and Language Development: Some Key Issues. In J. Orasanu (ed.) *Reading Comprehension: From Research to Practice*. Hillsdale, NJ: Lawrence Erlbaum Associates.

Heath, S. B. 1982. What no bedtime story means. *Language in Society* Vol. II:49–76.

———— 1983. *Ways With Words*. Cambridge: Cambridge University Press.

———— 1984. Literacy or literate skills: Considerations for ESL/EFL learners. In P. Larson, E. L. Judd, and D. S. Messerschmitt (eds.), *On Tesol 84*. Washington, DC: TESOL.

Hinds, J. 1987. Reader versus Writer Responsibility: A New Typology. In U. Connor and R. Kaplan, (eds.) *Writing Across Languages: Analysis of L2 Text*. Reading, MA: Addison-Wesley Publishing Company.

Hoffman, D. M. and Heath, S. B. 1986. *Inside Learners*. Stanford University, Stanford, CA.

Hosenfeld, C. 1977. A Preliminary Investigation of the Reading Strategies of Successful and Unsuccessful Second Language Learners. *System* Vol. 5, #2.

Hudelson, S. 1981. *Learning to Read in Different Languages*. Washington, DC: Center for Applied Linguistics.

Hudson, T. 1980. The effects of induced schemata on the "short circuit" in L2 reading performance, *Language Learning* Vol. 32, #1.

Hymes, D. 1981. *"In vain I tried to tell you"*: Essays in Native American Ethnopoetics. Philadelphia: University of Pennsylvania Press.

Johns, A. 1981. Necessary English: A Faculty Survey. *TESOL Quarterly* Vol. 15, #1.

Johnston, P. H. 1983. *Reading Comprehension Assessment: A Cognitive Basis*. Newark, DE: International Reading Association.

Kaplan, R. 1966. Cultural Thought Patterns and Intercultural Education. *Language Learning* Vol 16, #1 & 2.

———— 1987. Cultural Thought Patterns Revisited. In U. Connor and R. Kaplan, (eds.), *Writing Across Languages: Analysis of L2 Text*. Reading, MA: Addison-Wesley Publishing Company.

Kintsch, W. 1974. *The Representation of Meaning in Memory* New York: Wiley.

———— 1977. On Comprehending Stories. In M. Just and P. Carpenter (eds.), *Cognitive Processes in Comprehension*. Hillsdale, NJ: Lawrence Erlbaum Associates.

Kintsch, W. and Van Dijk, T. A. 1978. Toward a model of text comprehension and production. *Psychology Review* Vol. 85(5):363–394.

Kolers, P. A. 1973. Three Stages of Reading, in F. Smith (ed.) *Psycholinguistics and Reading*. New York: Holt, Rinehart and Winston.

Krashen, S. 1985. *Insights and Inquiries*. Hayward, CA: Alemany Press.

Langer, J. A. 1981. From Theory to Practice: A Pre-reading Plan. *Journal of Reading* Vol. 25:452.

Langer, J. A. (ed.) 1987. *Language, Literacy, and Culture: Issues of Society and Schooling*. Norwood, NJ: Ablex Publishing Company.

Long, M. and Richards, J. C. 1987. *Methodology in TESOL*. New York: Newbury House Publishers.

Mackay, R., Barkman, B. and Jordan R. R., (eds.) 1979. *Reading in a Second Language: Hypotheses, Organization, and Practice*. Rowley, MA: Newbury House Publishers.

Mahon. D. 1986. Intermediate Skills: Focusing on Reading Rate Development. In F. Dubin, D. E. Eskey, and W. Grabe (eds) *Teaching Second Language Reading for Academic Purposes* (eds.). Reading, MA: Addison-Wesley Publishing Company.

Mandler, J. 1984. *Stories, Scripts, and Scenes: Aspects of Schema Theory*. Hillsdale, NJ: Lawrence Erlbaum Associates.

McNeil, J. D. 1987. *Reading Comprehension: New Directions for Classroom Practice*. Second Edition. Glenview, IL: Scott, Foresman and Company.

McNeil, J. D. and Donant, L. 1982. Summarizing strategy for improving reading comprehension. In J. Niles and L. Miller (eds.). *New Inquiries in Reading Research Instruction*, 31st Yearbook of the National Reading Conference. Rochester, NY: The National Reading Conference.

Meyer, B. 1977. The Structure of Prose: Effects on Learning and Memory and Implication for Educational Practice. In R. C. Anderson, R. J. Spiro, and W. E. Montague, (eds.) *Schooling and the Acquisition of Knowledge*. Hillsdale, NJ: Lawrence Erlbaum Associates.

Meyer, B. and Rice, E. 1987. The interaction of reader strategies and the organization of text. *Text* Vol. 2, #1–3.

Michaels, S. 1986. Narrative presentations: An Oral Preparation for Literacy with First Graders. In J. Cook-Gumperz (ed.), *The Social Construction of Literacy*. Cambridge: Cambridge University Press.

Mikulecky, B. 1984. Reading Skills Instruction in ESL. In P. Larson, E. L. Judd, and D. S. Messerschmitt (eds.) *On TESOL '84*. Washington, DC: TESOL.

Mikulecky, E. 1984. Unpublished seminar paper, Boston University.
———— 1985. Unpublished seminar paper, Boston University.

Nagy, W. E., Herman, P, and Anderson, R. 1985. Learning Words from Context. *Reading Research Quarterly* Vol. 20, #2.

Nespor, J. 1987. The Construction of School Knowledge: A Case Study. *Journal of Education* Vol. 169:34–54.

Nuttall, C. 1982. *Teaching Reading Skills in a Foreign Language*. London: Heinemann Educational Books.

Olshavsky, J. 1976. Reading as problem solving: an investigation of strategies. *Reading Research Quarterly* Vol. 12, #4.

Olsen, M. 1982. Paper presented at ESL Symposium, Newton, MA.

Olson, D. R. 1977. From Utterance to Text: The Bias of Language in Speech and Writing. *Harvard Education Review* Vol. 47.

Ong, W. 1982. *Orality and Literacy: The Technologizing of the Word*. London: Methuen.

Orasanu, J. (ed.) 1986. *Reading Comprehension: From Research to Practice*. Hillsdale, NJ: Lawrence Erlbaum Associates.

Ostler, S. 1987. English in Parallels: A Comparison of English and Arabic Prose. In U. Connor and R. Kaplan, (eds.) *Writing Across Languages: Analysis of L2 Text*. Reading, MA: Addison-Wesley Publishing Company.

Palinscar, A. S. and Brown, A. L. 1985. Reciprocal teaching of comprehension monitoring activities. In J. Osborn., P. Wilson, and R. C. Anderson, (eds.). *Reading Education: Foundations for a Literate America*. Lexington, MA: Lexington Books.

Pattison, Robert, 1982. *On Literacy: The Politics of the Word from Homer to the Age of Rock*. Oxford: Oxford University Press.

Pearson, P. D. (ed.) 1984. *A Handbook of Reading Research*. New York: Longman.

Pica, T., Young, R. and Doughty, C. 1987. The Impact of Interaction on Comprehension. *TESOL Quarterly* Vol. 21, #4.

Raatz, U. and Klein-Braley, C. 1984. The C-Test — A Modification of the Cloze Procedure. In T. Culhane, C. Klein-Braley, and D. Stevenson (eds.), *Occasional Papers: Practice and Problems in Language Testing*. Cochester, England:University of Essex.

Reynolds, R. E., Taylor, M. A., Steffensen, M. S., Shirey, L. L. and Anderson, R. C. 1982. Cultural Schemata and Reading Comprehension. *Reading Research Quarterly* Vol. 17.

Rumelhart, D. E. 1980. Schemata: the building blocks of cognition. In R. J. Spiro, B. C. Bruce, and W. F. Brewer, (eds.), *Theoretical Issues in Reading Comprehension*. Hillsdale, NJ: Lawrence Erlbaum Associates.

Rumelhart, D. E. and Ortony, A. 1977. The representation of knowledge in memory. In R. C. Anderson, R. J. Spiro, and W. E. Montague (eds.), *Schooling and the Acquisition of Knowledge*. Hillsdale, NJ: Lawrence Erlbaum Associates.

Samuels, S. J. and Kamil, M. L. 1984. Models of the Reading Process. In D. Pearson (ed.) *Handbook of Reading Research*. New York: Longman.

Schank, R. C. and Abelson, R. C. 1977. *Scripts, Plans, Goals, and Understanding*. Hillsdale, NJ: Lawrence Erlbaum Associates.

Schieffelin, B. and Cochran-Smith, M. 1984. Learning to Read Culturally: Literacy Before Schooling, in H. Goelman, A. Oberg, and F. Smith (eds.), *Awakening to Literacy*. Portsmouth, NH: Heinemann Educational Books.

Schieffelin, B. and Ochs, E. 1986. Language Socialization. *Annual Review of Anthropology* Vol. 15.

Schlessinger, J. H. 1984. Outside Reading and Oral Reports: Sure-fire Reading Motivation. *Journal of Reading* Vol. 28, #3.

Schulz, R. A. 1983. From word to meaning: foreign language reading instruction after the elementary course. *The Modern Language Journal* Vol. 67(2):127–134.

Scollon R., and Scollon, S. 1981. *Narrative, Literacy, and Face in Interethnic Communication*. Norwood, NJ: Ablex Publishing Company.

Scribner, S. and Cole, M. 1981. *The Psychology of Literacy*. Cambridge, MA: Harvard University Press.

Sivell, J. N. 1987. Profile of the ESL extensive reader. Paper presented at the 21st Annual Convention of TESOL. April 21–25, 1987. Miami, Florida.

Smith, F. (ed.) 1973. *Psycholinguistics and Reading*. New York: Holt, Rinehart and Winston.

Smith, F. 1986. *Understanding Reading (Third Ed.)* Hillsdale, NJ: Lawrence Erlbaum Associates.

Smith, S. 1984. *The Theater Arts and the Teaching of Second Languages*. Reading, MA: Addison-Wesley Publishing Company.

Stanovich, K. E. 1980. Toward an interactive-compensatory model of individual differences in the development of reading fluency. *Reading Research Quarterly* Vol. 16, #1.

Steffenson, M. S., Joag-dev, C. and Anderson, R. C. 1979. A Cross-cultural Perspective on Reading Comprehension. *Reading Research Quarterly* Vol. 15.

Stein, N. L. 1986. Critical issues in the development of literacy education: toward a theory of learning and instruction. In N. Stein, (ed.) *Literacy in American Schools: Learning to Read and Write*. Chicago: University of Chicago Press.

Stein, N. L. and Trabasso, T. 1982. What's in a Story: An Approach to Comprehension and Instruction. In R. Glaser, (ed.) *Advances in Instructional Psychology, Volume 2*. Hillsdale, NJ: Lawrence Erlbaum Associates.

Stoller, F. 1986. Reading Lab: Developing Low-level Reading Skills. In F. Dubin, D. Eskey, and W. Grabe (eds.). *Teaching Second Language Reading for Academic Purposes*. Reading, MA: Addison-Wesley Publishing Company.

Street, B. 1984. *Literacy in Theory and Practice*. Cambridge: Cambridge University Press.

Taylor, W. L. 1953. "Cloze procedure": a new tool for measuring readability. *Journalism Quarterly* Vol. 30:415–433.

Thorndike, R. L. 1974. Reading as reasoning. *Reading Research Quarterly*. Vol. 9.

Tierney, R. J. and Cunningham, J. W. 1984. Research on Teaching Reading Comprehension. In Pearson D. (ed.) *Handbook of Reading Research*. New York: Longman.

Van Daalen-Kapteijns, M. and Elshou-Mohr, M. 1981. The acquisition of word meaning as a cognitive learning process. *Journal of Verbal Learning and Verbal Behavior* Vol. 20:386–399.

Van Dijk, T. and Kintsch, W. 1983. *Strategies of Discourse Comprehension*. New York: Academic Press.

Vygotsky, L. S. 1962. *Thought and Language*. Cambridge, MA: Massachusetts Institute of Technology Press.

Wagner, D. 1987. Does Learning to Read in a Second Language Always Put the Child at a Disadvantage? Some Counter Evidence from Morocco. Paper presented at the 12th Annual Boston University Conference On Language Development. October 23–25, 1987. Boston, MA.

Watson-Gegeo, K. and Gegeo, D. 1986. *Language Socialization Across Cultures*. New York: Cambridge University Press.

Wertsch, J. V. (ed.) 1985. *Culture, Communication, and Cognition: Vygotskian Perspectives*. Cambridge: Cambridge University Press.

Widdowson, H. G. 1981. English for Specific Purposes: Criteria for Course Design. In L. Selinker, et. al. (eds.) *English for Academic and Technical Purposes*. Rowley, MA: Newbury House Publishers.

Winograd, T. 1977. A Framework for Understanding Discourse, in M. A. Just and P. A. Carpenter (eds.), *Cognitive Processes in Comprehension*. Hillsdale, N.J.: Lawrence Erlbaum Associates.

Zupnik, J-Y. 1988. In B. Mikulecky and J-Y. Zupnik, Teaching Reading Skills. Paper presented at the 22nd Annual TESOL Convention. March 9, 1988, Chicago, IL.

Classroom Materials Cited

Bander, R. G. 1980. *From Sentence to Paragraph*. New York: Holt, Rinehart and Winston.

Bonesteel, L. 1986. Unpublished curriculum materials, Harvard University.

Connelly, M. and Sims. J. 1982. *Time and Space: A Basic Reader*. Englewood Cliffs, NJ: Prentice-Hall, Inc.

Fry, E. B. 1978. *Reading Drills for Speed and Comprehension*. Providence, RI: Jamestown Publishers.

———— 1978. *Skimming and Scanning, Advanced Level*. Providence, RI: Jamestown Publishers.

Furbrush, P., Ross, E, and Durrell, D. 1975. *Thirty Lessons in Outlining Level 1*. North Billerica, MA. Curriculum Associates.

Graham, C. 1978. *Jazz Chants*. New York: Oxford University Press.

Harris, D. P. 1966. *Reading Improvement Exercises for Students of English as a Second Language*. Englewood Cliffs, NJ: Prentice-Hall, Inc.

Joffee, I. L. 1984. *Opportunity for Skillful Reading*. 4th Edition. Belmont, CA: Wadsworth Publishing Co.

Krantz, H., Kimmelman, J., Seltzer, S., Martin, C., Sackmary, R.,and Lantz-Goldhaber, S. 1981. *Discovering American English: Reading*. New York: Macmillan and Company.

Mikulecky, B. and Jeffries, L. 1986. *Reading Power*. Reading, MA: Addison-Wesley Publishing Company.

Moore, J. et. al. 1979. *Reading and Thinking in English*. Oxford: Oxford University Press.

Motta, J. and Riley, K. 1982. *Impact! Adult Literacy and Language Skills, Books 1 and 2 and Teacher's Guide*. Reading, MA: Addison-Wesley Publishing Company.

Niles, O. et. al. 1965. *Tactics in Reading. I, II, and III*. Glenview, IL.: Scott, Foresman and Company.

Parker, D. H. 1973. *Reading Laboratory Kit 3a*. Chicago, IL: Science Research Associates, Inc.

Ross, E. and Culliton, T. 1971. *Thirty Lessons in Outlining: Advanced*. North Billerica, MA: Curriculum Associates.

Shostak, M. 1981. *NISA: The Life and Words of a !Kung Woman*. New York: Vintage Books

Sonka, A. L. 1981. *Skillful Reading*. Englewood Cliffs, NJ: Prentice-Hall, Inc.

Spargo, E. and Williston, G. R. 1980. *Timed Readings*. Providence, RI: Jamestown Publishers.

Thurstone, T. G. 1965. *Reading For Understanding*. Chicago, IL: Science Research Associates.

Variety Word-find Puzzles. May, 1988. Vol. 31, #5. New York: Official Publications, Inc.

Index

Meghan R. Norenberg
3/514-5097

Meghan R. Norenberg